T H E
WIDE OPEN
DOOR

THE
WIDE OPEN
DOOR

My conversation with God
in the Operating Room

Neeraj Bhushan, M.D.

To order additional copies of this book, contact:
Xlibris Corporation
1-888-795-4274
www.Xlibris.com
Orders@Xlibris.com
53003

Acknowledgements

This book comes to my readers through the blessings of "Bapu" whose Spiritual inspirations kept my pen flowing in the darkest moments.

Special thanks to my editor Lois Gilbert for her guidance and my friend Vikram Khushalani for his encouragement.

To my dear wife Manju for her patience
and my mother for her support.

Contents

Chapter 1

JOURNEY OF FAITH

Anxiety and panic choked me. I became aware of fine beads of sweat on my forehead and a prickling in my armpits, although my hands and feet were ice-cold. The wheels of the gurney seemed to move slowly, inch-by-inch, and then sped up until I felt as though we were traveling a mile a minute. Above me I could see bright ceiling lights and faces looking down at me. Terrified of the ordeal that lay before me, knowing too well what to expect, I could feel my muscles tense with the desire to stop the forward motion of the gurney.

The odor of the hospital hallways seemed so different, yet so familiar. I walked these areas of the hospital every day as a physician, but now I was just another patient, being wheeled down to the operating room for the surgical repair of my left knee.

Even though I'd witnessed the favorable outcome of this surgical procedure hundreds of times in the past twenty-five years, the occasions when it didn't go so well completely preoccupied me. This sense of impending doom was interrupted by the loud whoosh of the double doors, which flung open to the operating suite a few feet away.

The gurney stopped with a hiss of rubber, and the sound also stopped my chain of thoughts. I heard a commotion in the OR suite from the personnel inside who were preparing the room for my surgery. Now I was alone with my fear, and I was scared shitless. *Dr. B, you'll have no control over anything in a few minutes. You have always been in charge in your profession as a doctor, but not now. In a few moments you'll be completely sedated, motionless and unaware of your surroundings, as if you were dead. Oh my God, What am I doing here? I don't want this. Someone, please help me. Please. I'm scared. Please help me.*

Chapter 2

INJURY

On a beautiful Saturday afternoon in the summer of 1995, my son Alex invited some of his high school friends to our house to play basketball. On one end of the driveway, the basketball hoop stood next to the garage. I watched these three teenagers enjoying a friendly game. I played basketball with Alex often, and this afternoon he invited me to join them. Initially, I hesitated—I'm in my forties, and I wondered whether it would be prudent to play with these young kids. But I played basketball and soccer for my school team while growing up, and competed in inter-school tournaments. I wasn't going to let these young guys have all the fun. I'd give them a game to remember.

We played for half an hour, and during the last few minutes of the game, I went for a rebound. Since I'm only five foot six inches tall, I had to leap high for the ball, and when I came down I twisted the left knee. Immediately I knew something had given way, and the pain increased by the minute. I decided not to talk about it, finished the game, told them that I had a lot of fun and I needed a drink of water.

By night time my left knee was aching and swollen. My wife Manju saw me applying an ice pack to the knee and said "What happened? Why are you applying this ice pack?"

"I twisted my knee while I was playing basketball with Alex and his buddies."

"Does it hurt a lot? What can I do to help? I see it swelling up. May be some Ibuprofen would help."

I took a tablet of ibuprofen and went to bed, hoping the analgesic would give me relief. I knew Manju would worry about me, so of course I wanted to downplay the extent of my pain and injury. In the morning, I noted some improvement. The treatment with ice and anti-inflammatory medicine helped. I repeated it for next three or four days and my knee felt better. Eventually I returned to my usual routine of jogging, and enjoyed an active lifestyle.

Running in the park has always been my favorite exercise. We have a park with a jogging trail and a community center close to our house, and I liked to run three or four miles at least twice a week. Within a few weeks, however, the injury during the basketball game started to affect my jogging. My knee began to ache every time I exercised, and sometimes it would swell up. Going up the stairs felt uncomfortable. I knew there would be trouble ahead with this knee.

I decided not to disclose the problem to Manju, at least for the moment. After eighteen years of marriage, I knew better than to invite a lecture and get into an argument with her. She has never been thrilled with my jogging obsession, and I knew she would be upset knowing my knee was worse after my usual running routine. Like most men, I wanted to deal with the problem on my own terms. Of course this didn't work.

One day she saw me walking with a slight limp. "You don't listen!" she said. "You just have to jog. Why can't you find some other form of exercise?"

"Okay, okay. I'll."

"I want you to get that knee checked. You don't want this pain to linger."

I set up an appointment to see my colleague, orthopedic surgeon Dr. Walter the following week. As I drove to his office, I wondered, *What's wrong with my knee? Will it be a torn meniscus, degenerative arthritis or a torn ligament? Will it need surgery?*

The human mind can run off in a fraction of a second, and fly thousands of miles in a moment. It can trap us in pessimism and make us miserable. Being a doctor didn't make it any easier—in fact, it made things worse. I know too much about all that can go wrong. I am trained to. All my life, I have been taking a negative and turning it into a positive with healing, but now I was in pain and I couldn't change it by giving my own expert advice. I would have to rely on another doctor to take care of me. Even though I knew precisely how to fix the damaged knee on paper, I couldn't do it myself.

I wanted the knee to look perfect after the repair, the way it appeared in the anatomy book. I pictured the best illustrations and drawings. Would the orthopedic surgeon be able to do that? Would he be that meticulous, careful and concerned for me? Maybe. He performed operations every day and had been doing it for years. *In his eyes I'm just another patient coming down the assembly line. If he's not careful, or he's having a bad day . . . what if he's having family problems? Will he damage my knee even more? What if it gets worse than before?*

But I knew that Dr. Walter was a respectable surgeon—a knowledgeable, professional, no-nonsense kind of doctor. Besides, he worked right next door to my office, in the Pavilion building attached to the hospital. *But what if I don't really need surgery?* The possibilities of what could go wrong drowned me in a sea of negative thoughts.

Deep in my inner debate, I finally reached his office, signed the appointment book and sat down, waiting for my turn. The nurse called my name and escorted me into an exam room.

"Hey Neeraj, How are you? What brings you here?" Dr. Walter asked as he entered the exam room.

"Tom, I injured my knee playing basketball last week."

"Who do you play with? Do you play on a regular basis?"

"I played with my son and his buddies. It got quite intense."

"How old is he?"

"Sixteen." I said.

"What did you say? *Sixteen . . .*" He looked at me from above the top of his eyeglasses. That one look said it all, as clearly as if he'd spoken out loud. *Are you crazy? What are you doing playing with teenagers? Have you lost your mind?*

I smiled and shrugged. "I know."

"Let me examine your knee." He maneuvered my knee joint, checking flexion, extension, and weight bearing capacity. "It looks like a torn medial meniscus."

My heart sank. "Are you sure, Tom?"

"I am fairly certain, but let's get an MRI scan to confirm it. I'll write you a prescription for an anti-inflammatory medicine. Do you exercise on a regular basis?"

"Yes! I jog."

"No running till I see you again with the MRI films."

"Okay, Tom. Thank you." I smiled in an attempt to cover my dismay and walked out of his office.

Torn meniscus! Oh my God, my jogging days are over. Maybe it will need surgery. Why is this happening to me? I've tried to take care of myself, exercise regularly and keep my weight under control. Depressed and frustrated that I wouldn't be able to run again, I consoled myself one moment and then felt enraged the next, weaving through an emotional roller coaster. Reluctantly, feeling the emotional toll of not knowing what lay ahead, I scheduled the MRI scan.

The injury to my knee reminded me of other family problems. I'd witnessed sickness and death with my brother and father, and my mind drifted into the past to relive the agony suffered by my loved ones. Maybe it was instinctive to look for comfort there, a way to forget my own physical setback and think about my brother and my dad.

Chapter 3

DREAMS

When my older brother was nineteen years old, he died from a ruptured aneurysm in his brain, caused by malignant hypertension. I was thirteen years old at the time, and I saw how his loss devastated my parents. To provide them with the emotional support they needed, I had to hide my own grief for many years.

I left home at the age of seventeen to go to Medical school. Life on the Medical school campus was a lot of hard work, but I spent a lot of time with my parents. I dreamt of finishing my education and establishing myself as a practicing physician, so I could help them in their older years. I saw my dad work very hard to put my brother through engineering school, and he did the same to pay for my education in medical school. I wanted to repay him for all his years of sacrifice. Sadly, that opportunity was taken away from me when he passed away at the age of sixty, in India, while I was in my first year of internship in the United States. I never had the chance to spend time with him or care for him in his last months. That created a void in my life for years.

Dad came from a large family of three brothers and four sisters, and he was born in the middle of the pack. He grew up in a small farming town in the western part of India, which is now in Pakistan. His dream as he was growing up was to get a college education and move to the capital city, New Delhi. For many years his devotion to his family kept him from pursuing his dream to relocate. This was in the 1930's, and with eight children in the family and his father's paltry income, supporting a large family meant he had to live with extremely limited resources.

One day he confided in his older sister about his intention to move to New Delhi and how the lack of resources to make the move bothered him. She loved him dearly and gave him ten rupees—equivalent to two dollars at that time—from the little money she had saved. It cost six rupees to travel by train to New Delhi. His uncle lived in the city where he worked as a civil engineer for the Department of Housing and Urban Development. He had promised my father a place to stay, as well as financial help with college tuition. Finally at the age of twenty, Dad landed in the big city he had always dreamt about. The first thing he did was to join a college to learn English. Britain ruled India at that time, so Dad worked hard to become proficient in the English language, which helped him find a job in The Department of Defense. He started at the entry level position, but honesty, hard work and commitment propelled him to higher ranks. He earned the respect and admiration of his peers early in his career.

I always found him leaving for work early in the morning and returning late in the evening. He taught me to work hard, be honest and get the best education possible. I sailed through the school as an A student and won admission to a prestigious medical school in 1969. Around that time, dad was diagnosed with high blood pressure. In my second year of medical school, Dad started to feel weak and tired and lost six pounds from his already diminutive frame. His evaluation revealed he had developed a mild kidney failure, secondary to his high blood pressure. Our family doctor painted a bleak picture of this new development and told us that Dad would probably die within five or six years. My mother was crushed by the news. She was only forty-eight years old at the time. The doctor prescribed a conservative treatment for the hypertension and chronic renal failure, which was the only medical option at the time. Dialysis was in the embryonic stage of development, and kidney transplants were unheard of. I started reading about high blood pressure and kidney disease in my medical textbooks to find anything that could help my dad.

Dad maintained a reasonable life style for the next three years and retired from the government at the age of fifty-eight in 1975. I finished medical school the same year. One day I sat with my dad and told him I wanted to go to United States for further studies. That day, Dad told me about his dream and how he had migrated from a small village to the big city. I knew money was tight and I didn't want to encumber my parents, but he encouraged me to pursue my dream. When I told him I didn't want to be a burden, he only smiled and said "We'll manage."

I passed the medical and English exam and emigrated to the United States in January 1977. At that time, there was no direct phone connection back home. I had to book a call with the phone company and it took between twelve to twenty-four hours to get a connection. The cost was outrageous. The mail took six weeks to reach my parents.

A year later, just after I started my internship in the United States, I received an emergency phone call from a class fellow and a trusted friend, who said that Dad was in critical condition. He had developed a urinary tract infection for which he was prescribed strong antibiotic injections. This drug was toxic to the kidney and in seven days he had slipped into renal coma. He was transferred to the University hospital. I knew my father was deteriorating slowly, but I didn't expect his collapse would happen so soon. My professor, the Director of Medicine, was kind enough to grant me two weeks leave to go and visit my dying father.

As soon as Manju and I reached New Delhi, we went straight to the hospital to see him. Dad had been given emergency dialysis, and he was in a semi comatose state, barely responsive and didn't recognize me. I was overwhelmed with emotion when I saw him in that condition. Only a year earlier, he had been alert, upright and vibrant and now I stood in a hospital facing the death of my beloved father.

Miraculously, Dad woke up three days later, after two sessions of dialysis. He was delighted to see me, and we talked for what seemed to be a long time but was actually less than an hour. He even asked to see the newspaper, which was one of his favorite things to read. He asked me a lot of questions that day about my life in United States.

"How is your residency coming along?"

"I work long hours, Dad, but that's expected. I have two more years of training left." We talked about the excellence of American medicine and American medical technology.

"How is your apartment?"

"We have a one bedroom apartment, enough for Manju and me. It's on the third floor of a building in a nice area. About twenty five minutes commute to the hospital."

Manju and I had just wed, and he asked, "How is Manju? Are both of you happy together?"

"Yes. We are. I miss you and Mom a lot. It's so far away."

"I know. We'll be together soon. You concentrate on your training."

"Dad, how are you feeling?"

"I feel weak. My appetite is gone."

"I can see you've lost weight. You'll feel better after a few more sessions of dialysis. Don't give up, Dad. I'll finish my training and come back after two years."

"I love you, my boy."

"I love you too, Dad."

That was the last conversation I had with him.

I had to leave him with a heavy heart. I had already extended my leave by another week and could not get any more time off. I knew he was terminal and the time was running out. I returned to the United States and a week later, Dad passed away from complications of dialysis. I was torn between two countries, after starting my life in America and then losing my father back in India. For the next few months I lived in despair. Even today, a feeling of desolation strikes me when I think of my father. He was a good and caring man, and I never had the chance to serve him, love him and be with him when he needed me the most.

Life has its own agenda and timetable. The end of his journey marked a new beginning for me. In the midst of my crazy schedule and long hours of training, the memory of his physical death vanished like smoke. But during my solitary moments, the fact of his death came roaring back to the forefront of my awareness. In those days I always felt rushed, and the daily pressure to perform meant I never had time to grieve fully for his loss. Eventually the grief felt locked in me forever. Even today, after twenty eight years, the memory of our final conversation leaves me with a feeling of melancholy.

Chapter 4

MRI

The MRI technician told me the test would take approximately twenty minutes and I would hear the loud sounds of the magnets. I had to lie perfectly still on a stretcher that slid into a tubular structure, with the curved interior ceiling barely three inches above my face. It reminded me of a coffin. For a claustrophobic person, it could be nerve-wracking. The scan started and sure enough it produced loud, annoying noises: *tick tick-tick ka-tick*. The noise came from small hammers striking against a metal surface, and while the sound was sometimes rhythmic, it was also haphazard. I felt relieved when it was over.

"We're done. I hope it wasn't too uncomfortable for you." the tech said as she pulled the stretcher out of the machine that had swallowed me. "You can go ahead and change. I'll take the films to the radiologist when they're ready. It should take about an hour. You can come back and pick up the films then."

I scheduled my appointment with Dr. Walter for the following day. I was nervous and fidgety as I sat in the waiting room of his office with the MRI films, and I wanted to see him quickly. I was anxious to hear what he had to tell me. Maybe the meniscus was really bad and I needed surgery right away. Or maybe physical therapy and rest would relieve my pain. I hoped there would be a simple remedy, and my jogging days were not over yet. I picked up a magazine and opened it without seeing it, lost in my thoughts until the nurse opened the door and called, "Dr. Bhushan?"

I dropped the magazine back on the table and stood. "Yes."

"Hi, I'm Karen. Please follow me into the exam room. How are you, Dr. Bhushan?"

"I am fine. I messed up my knee playing basketball."

"Did you get the MRI?"

"Yes, it was done yesterday. Here are the films."

She took them from me and smiled reassuringly. "Good. I'll place them on the view box for Dr. Walter. He'll be in shortly."

"Thanks Karen." I sat down on the chair.

Dr. Walter walked in five minutes later, "Hi Neeraj, How are you today?"

"I'm feeling better but my knee is still sore."

"Let me see what's going on with your knee." He turned his attention to the images on the view box. "There's a small tear in the medial meniscus." He pointed to the scan. "Here it is."

A tear! My jogging days are over, I thought.

"It's not bad. It's small and should mend with rest, therapy and anti-inflammatory medicines. You don't need surgery now." Dr. Walter's words were reassuring.

"Thank goodness" I said.

"You may need to have it surgically repaired in the future. When, we don't know. Menisci do wear down with age."

"I am glad to know this. I will be careful and not push myself. Thanks for your time, Dr. Walter. But when can I run again?"

He looked at me with an understanding smile. "Wait for at least a month. Walking might be better for your knee. Perhaps light jogging would be okay after a while. Be careful though."

It was comforting to get this report, but I knew this problem was going to come back and haunt me. I had a ticking time bomb in my knee.

It could have been a lot worse. I started my therapy and medicines and the knee started to feel better after a couple of weeks. A month later, it was almost back to normal. Gradually, I resumed my light jogging routine, though not as vigorously as before. There was always a shadow over the pleasure it gave me because I knew the findings on the MRI scan.

Months passed by. One day, after I ran, the pain in my knee returned. A few days of rest helped my knee and it felt better. I am stubborn; like most men. *Hey, come on now, it's me. No one can tell me to slow down.* I started jogging again. A few days went by and my knee started to hurt, even when I was walking. I was afraid to tell this to any one, particularly Manju.

She knew I was jogging and was not happy about it. Every time she saw me putting on my sneakers and jogging trunks, she frowned and shook her head. "Why are you doing this? Why can't you just walk, or ride the stationary bike?" This discussion always ended in an argument. This time, I knew she'd been right. *Face it, Raj: she was right and I was wrong.* Defeat was headed my way, and that was not acceptable to me. I was in constant pain and I knew I had no choice. Finally, I broke the news to Manju.

She looked at me, didn't say a word for a minute, looked away and then back at me again. I smiled and said, "You know my dear, I have been careful. What can I do? I love to run. I guess I will have to stop."

"I have been telling you, but you don't listen," she said. "Show me where it hurts." Even though I knew she was concerned, she told me not to worry. "I will massage your knee. Take some anti-inflammatory medicines for a few days and you'll be fine."

She has magic in her hands. Three days of massage relieved the pain enough for me to walk without much discomfort. I decided to refrain from jogging for a month. After six weeks, I was still reluctant to run. Internally, I was afraid of the torn meniscus. *It can't heal by itself. Will it get worse as I get older? Bodies go through a slow deterioration process as we grow old. Should I abstain from jogging altogether?* Perhaps the knee would heal if I had faith. I must have faith, I thought, though I still felt doubt. I floated in between faith and doubt, waiting for my aching knee to be healed.

Chapter 5

SPIRITUAL RAPTURE

For the first ten years after finishing the medical school, I practiced medicine as a solo practitioner, virtually on call every day and every night. Imagine what that's like: you're just dozing off when a call from the emergency room wakes you up at midnight. One of your patients has come in to the hospital with chest pain. What do you do? After doing whatever you can over the phone, you get up, change into your work clothes, put your jacket on, pick up your briefcase, head towards the garage, and go to the hospital. The five minutes it takes to change and leave home are tough, but once in the car, driving to the hospital, it all changes. Now you're focused on that patient.

How is he doing? I better get there quickly. That patient needs me.

A little after midnight, I park my car and walk into the hospital. As I walk down the brightly lit long hallways, all I hear is the sound of my shoes. I come in through a dead silent long hallway to the rear entrance of the ER, an area where death and disease are thwarted by the fury of medical personnel and technology. This world never sleeps; on the contrary, they are wide-awake and completely impervious to the still darkness of the outside world.

The activity of the hospital employees bursts on my senses once I enter through the double doors of the Emergency. I can hear a child's loud cry from one of the exam room on the left. A strong fecal smell rises from another exam room, while urine emanates from the next. Feeling queasy, I walk briskly to the other side of the nursing station. This is closest to the ambulance entrance and is used for the critical patients. As I enter, the paramedics have just brought in a man who is wheeled in on a gurney, undergoing CPR. The ER doctor and two nurses are working on him. Another nurse runs to get the red crash cart as he is taken into the last unoccupied exam room and the drapes are drawn. The ER is packed today and nurses, technicians and the doctors are all busy with emergencies.

Directly in front of the entrance is an inverted U shaped nursing station, littered with computers, monitors, phones, patient's charts, admission paperwork and medicines. There is an EKG machine and a red crash cart with IV medicines, ambo bag, nasal cannula and a defibrillator. These are kept on either side of the nursing station. The three exam rooms on the right are all occupied with patients and family members.

I check the white board on the back wall of the nursing station to get the room number for Mr. Smith. Entering his exam room, I see a man in his fifties, somewhat obese, lying on a stretcher. He is distressed with chest pain, his vitals displayed on the monitor. A rubber tube has been placed in his nostrils and twisted around the ears to keep it in place and supply the life-saving oxygen. He is on intravenous blood thinner and getting other IV medications and being closely monitored by the nurse. The monitor shows normal heart rhythm. Electrocardiogram tracing shows ST segment elevation in the inferior and lateral portion of the heart muscle. This type of electrocardiogram change is an ominous sign of heart attack. A typical full cycle of a single heartbeat has different components for the contraction and relaxation of the heart. These are termed as various intervals of the heartbeat. They are PR interval, QRS interval and ST interval.

Looking at the EKG changes tells me that this man's poor heart muscle is crying for more blood and oxygen. The EKG clearly shows the impediment to the much needed blood flow. The man's face breaks out in a cold sweat as his heart struggles for blood and oxygen. Death looms over his ashen face, due to the lack of oxygen. An uncomfortable aura of impending doom hovers over him, even though the Cardio Pulmonary resuscitation crash cart with defibrillator is sitting by the bedside. Things can change at a moment's notice.

Life can slip away in a matter of minutes, right in front of your eyes.

I keep my composure and examine the patient, whose color improves a bit. I review all the laboratory tests before I ask him, "Jim, How are you feeling?"

"Dr. B, my chest pain is much better, almost gone."

"That's good. I am glad to hear that." I make an effort to stay calm, although the tests don't look good. "Jim, the EKG is suspicious for heart attack. We are waiting for additional blood tests to confirm it."

The stress of the last few hours has taken its toll on his face. He takes a deep breath and holds it as he struggles to accept the news. He exhales without a complaint.

"Dr. B, What are you checking in the blood?"

"We check the level of damaged heart muscle in the blood. These are called cardiac enzymes."

"When will you know for sure, Dr. B.?"

"We need at least three blood tests, two hours apart. By early morning we'll have more information. If you have any more chest pain, we need to know right away."

"Yes, Dr. B. I'll tell the nurse."

Any examination of a patient with chest pain—heart attack in this particular case or any other serious illness in the emergency room is extremely important. That is the first glimpse of a life threatening condition. Face to face contact itself will yield valuable information about that individual and family. My mentor, Dr. Henry, was a top notch bedside diagnostician. Not much else was available in technology in 1970's. There were no CT scans. MRI's were unheard of. No digital laboratory tests existed. A heart attack patient was given painkillers and observed in the Intensive Care Unit for days, and many times they did not make it. There was nothing else to do except pray and reassure the patient.

Back then the diagnosis was principally formed by a thorough bedside examination of the patient. Usually I met the patient in the ER to go over the whole history with a fine-tooth comb. Prompt evaluation and treatment of the patient is the key to the outcome of the illness.

When I first look at the patient, I ask myself, does he look healthy or sick? How is his color? Do the eyes have a spark in them or are they dull and glazed? Are the lips pink or dusky? Is the skin smooth, dry or moist? Then I examine the pulse. Quite often, I have made a diagnosis just by doing all that, thanks to Dr. Henry's teaching. A thready weak pulse is an ominous sign, while a strong bounding regular pulse is reassuring. Low blood pressure is a bad sign that could indicate a level of damaged heart enzymes in the blood. There are many things to take into account before instituting the appropriate prescription with IV meds, blood thinner, oxygen, or taking the patient to the Cath Lab for emergency coronary angiogram and angioplasty. All these life-saving decisions can be made only when you see the patient as soon as they come to the ER.

Two hours went by.

The patient was stable.

Relieved, I touched his arm gently. "You rest now. I'll see you in the morning."

"Thanks, Dr. B."

When I walked out of the exam room, his wife followed me and tugged at my sleeve. "Dr. B, will he be okay?" I saw her eyes fill with tears. "Dr. B, I have been telling him to take it easy. He works too hard and has been under a lot of stress at work lately."

I put my hand on her shoulder. "Cindy, with God's Grace, he is stable. His tests show that he had a mild heart attack. He is getting all the appropriate medications and oxygen, and he's being closely monitored. The first twenty four to thirty six hours are critical. He'll be transferred to the Coronary Care Unit shortly, where he will be constantly monitored. I'll come back in the morning to see him again."

Her eyes welled up again and tears streamed down her face.

I continued, "Have faith. He will be all right."

"Dr. B, Thank you so much."

I slowly walked out of the emergency room, praying for Jim and Cindy. 'Dear Lord, I do what you guide me to do. Please help Jim and Cindy through this adversity.' Over the years, I formed a habit of praying for my patients and their families. I am not fully convinced that it helps, but I know for sure that it does no harm. It also gives me hope and a peace of mind.

By the time I drove back home, it was two in the morning.

At five a.m. I received another call about Mr. Smith's progress. His blood tests were stable. I breathed a sigh of relief, glad that I'd done what I could for him. Completely exhausted, I fell asleep.

My office manager called me at seven a.m., just as I was forcing myself out of bed to get ready to go to the office. "Dr. B., the first four patients have rescheduled. You can sleep in."

"Jackie, you must be kidding! Are you sure? Thanks for letting me know. I've had a rough night. Now I can sleep another hour." *Someone out there is looking after me. Is Almighty God intervening for my comfort?* Lying in bed, I feel the gentle touch of the Lord like a feather stroking my temple, telling me to rest for another hour. Joy radiates from the smile on my face to my aching legs, filling me with relief, as if new life is infused into my exhausted body. I relax mentally and physically and enjoy the extra hour of uninterrupted sleep.

Having my schedule rearranged like this doesn't always happen, but it often happens when I find myself in a bind, trapped from all sides and feeling helpless. Then prayer always comes to my rescue. Sometimes I don't notice these reminders from Almighty

God, that someone is looking out for me. Life is a testing ground for my faith. At times my faith is strong and solid, and other times, I doubt if anything like divine intervention exists.

Chapter 6

INJURY AGAIN

After being in private practice for twenty-five years, I decided to take Tuesday mornings off and start seeing patients at twelve-thirty p.m. On this particular Tuesday, as I sat at the kitchen table my gaze fell on the wall clock. It was nine-thirty a.m. The second hand of the clock moved one notch at a time and sixty of those movements completed one full minute, though is seemed it took forever. Then another minute rolled by slowly. Life is made up of moments like this, stacked on top of each other. And yet I can't recall where the years have vanished. Time flies at a blazing speed. Ten years rolled by as if in a blink of an eye. God gave me ten good years with the damaged left knee, but then my faith had to take another leap in the fall of 2005.

That morning I ate a light breakfast of cereal and milk, read the newspaper headlines and then went out for a walk. It was a beautiful fall day, and I glanced appreciatively at the deep blue sky with a few cirrus clouds overhead. A bright sunny day, fresh air . . . *Mmm, a crisp morning, perfect for a walk.* Each minute seemed to take hours, yet when I look back, years have flown by.

The leaves were changing color, from green to red, orange and yellow. Interposed in between these colors, some green was still visible, hanging on to the glory of spring and summer. I walked at a modest pace and saw a family of deer in the distance, a mama and papa deer and a little one. The fawn still had brown skin with white spots—probably no more than a few days old. Seeing me approach, they all darted across the asphalt road into the woods. Walking up the hilly terrain, I spotted a couple of squirrels and a rabbit. Playful, yet alert to my approach, they ran towards their hideout in a big tree. Watching nature's drama soothed my soul.

I came up to the top of the hill and made a left turn. This stretch of the road is relatively flat, so I picked up my pace to a brisk walk. Suddenly I felt a twinge in the inner part of my left knee. It soon increased in intensity. At first I ignored it and continued to walk, hoping it would subside. I started walking faster, trying to overcome the pain, but it steadily grew worse and slowed me down. Deep down, I knew I had a problem with the same knee that grounded me ten years ago. Even at a slower pace, the pain persisted. I turned around to go back but I was still quite a distance from home and in my misery it appeared much longer. Even though it was all down hill back to my home, it was still a quarter-mile away. My knee started to throb, reminding me of the knee injury ten years ago.

How our minds can change directions! Thirty minutes ago I had come out to walk and relax, and now I was worried about the pain in my knee. First I had to make it back. I knew Manju and my mother would find out, and start worrying. *I am not going to tell anyone. It will get better. Stop thinking too much Dr. B. It's just a knee pain. Take some anti-inflammatory medication. You're a doctor, so stop being a sissy.*

It must be my torn meniscus, acting up. Why did I have to walk fast? Couldn't I walk at a reasonable pace? You Macho man; see what you have done? You never listen. I scolded myself. As I came down the hill I went through a whirlwind of emotions. When I saw my house about hundred and fifty yards away, I breathed a sigh of relief. Now I knew I could make it.

Hey Raj, once you get home you can take some aspirin or Tylenol and you'll feel better. A hundred yards away from my front door, the pain jabbed me and I began to limp. *Oh boy, I'm in trouble. God please help me. Please get me home.* I hobbled through the next fifty yards and finally reached the end of the driveway. I stood there for five minutes and looked at my left knee. Externally, it looked fine. Slowly I walked to the side entrance of the house, contemplating my next move. I knew I had to put on a happy face for the two ladies waiting for me inside the house, even though I was in agony. I knew Manju and my mother would find out, and then there would be another lecture. *Hide as you might, somehow, your family always finds out. They know you too well. They have been with you for years.* Still, I didn't want to bother them even though I was in dire need of help, both emotionally and physically.

Slowly, gingerly I walked into the back door, not realizing they were both sitting at the kitchen table waiting for me.

"How was your walk?" Mom asked.

"Good. It's beautiful outside." I quickly grabbed a chair to sit down. Manju offered me a drink of water. I shifted my position on the chair and cringed as I felt a sharp pain in the knee.

Manju looked at me and asked, "Are you alright?"

Here it comes, I thought. "I'm fine. Just a little tired." I tried to get up and gasped before I fell back on the chair. "Ah!"

"Are you okay? What's the matter?" they asked.

I had no choice but to humbly say, "No, I'm not okay. My left knee hurts."

"Why? Did you fall?"

"No. It started to ache when I was walking."

"Did you jog today?"

"No,"

This answer was accepted with some skepticism.

"Really, I'm not lying. I was just walking."

"Let me see." Manju came around the table and looked at my knee. "It looks fine."

"The pain is deep inside," I said.

Her eyes widened in alarm, while her cheeks sagged and her lips quivered. "You don't rest enough. You work long hours. I have been telling you to take care of yourself. You just don't listen." And then, "Does it hurt a lot? What can I do to help? Here, put your leg up on the other chair."

Here you go again Dr. B, I thought, *Here comes the barrage of verbal thrashing along with love, concern and caring.* I listened to them for a few minutes and managed to escape the frenzy of advice about what to do, what not to do and what to take.

"Okay, I hear you both. I'll be careful." I promised them that I would get it evaluated by the orthopedist. Quietly I rose from the table, left the kitchen, took two tablets of Ibuprofen and got ready to go to work. I still had an office full of patients waiting for me.

Chapter 7

DIVINE INTERVENTION

I saw a patient in the office with swelling in her right leg. She had developed a blood clot, for which she was seen in the Emergency Room five days before. During the follow up visit in the office, her leg was still swollen. She appeared pale and exhausted, though not in any distress. She was on blood thinner injections—Lovenox as well as tablets—Coumadin. When she came into the office for a blood test, she was in a rush to leave and wouldn't stop talking on the cell phone. I sat her down and asked her if she was having any chest pains or shortness of breath.

"Dr. B, I'm feeling fine. I came in for a blood test. I'm closing on a property today, so I'm in a hurry. I have to make a few phone calls."

"Let me examine you before you go." I checked her pulse rate. It was one hundred twenty four. The normal pulse rate is sixty-to-eighty beats per minute. I told her to lie down so I could examine her and get an electrocardiogram. The EKG confirmed the rapid heartbeat.

"I am concerned about you. Fast heart beat or Tachycardia in the presence of a blood clot in the leg is an ominous sign of a blood clot in the lung." I advised her to get an emergency CT scan of the chest to make sure that she didn't have a pulmonary embolism.

Clearly annoyed, she stared at me as if I were crazy. "I don't feel bad, Dr. B. I have to go. I have some important things to take care of. What if I get the scan done tomorrow?"

"This is a serious matter," I insisted. "I'm concerned about you, Carmen. Blood clots in the lung can be fatal. I'll call the radiology department and schedule the CT scan for you right away."

She glowered at me for a moment, then reluctantly agreed. "Okay, Dr. B."

A few hours later she had an emergency CT angiogram of the chest. A large blood clot was discovered in her right lung. She was sent to the cardiac unit as an emergency admission for intravenous blood thinner. I went over to see her in the hospital later in the day. As I entered her room, she looked at me and said, "You saved my life, Dr. B." Her eyes filled with tears, her face flushed and she gulped air to hide her emotions. "Dr. B, I could have died. I was being silly, running around and not taking care of my health. You saved me." With tears rolling down her cheeks, she whispered, "Can I give you a hug?" She stretched her arms out.

I held one of her hands and put my arm around her shoulder and hugged her. I looked at her and said, "God saved your life, Carmen. I just did my job. We know what you have and you're getting the right treatment for it. You'll be fine."

I walked out of her room, blood rushing through my limbs, feeling lightheaded. *Wow!* I couldn't believe it. She did have a large blood clot in her right lung. She could have died.

Over the years, there have been many moments like this when I struggled to diagnose my patients, and guidance has come from above. When I feel that divine flow, it gives me the shivers. Sometimes I can hear the diagnosis in my mind as soon as I enter the exam room, before I've even looked at the patient. My eyes well up with tears then, especially when I haven't made any extra effort to diagnose a condition. Of course I try my best to figure out why and how this happens. And of course there is no way to know where this voice comes from. Not knowing, I just look up, smile and say, 'You helped me yet again. I know, Dear Lord. It can't be any other way.'

How can I take credit for this? How can I accept praise from others for my diagnostic acumen in treating the patients? *Oh! My Dear Lord, time and again, I know I have done nothing. This is not medical prowess—this is your guidance from within.*

Some may call it intuition, but I believe it is grace. God's Grace enters my brain and tells me the diagnosis of a condition promptly and accurately, often without even an examination. It is a Power that comes out of His Divine intervention and directs me to take the correct course of action. This Power is often seen by my patients as a unique ability to diagnose their problems, but I believe it is a Gift from the Almighty.

Repeatedly experiencing this over the years has made me a believer in the Supreme Power, in that Force, in my so-called intuition. I thanked God again for helping Carmen. She did not have any symptoms of chest pain or shortness of breath, and in my mind, her escape from certain death had to be a divine intervention.

I took several deep breaths and felt the electric current racing through my jumpy nerves begin to settle down. The warmth in my limbs returned and I felt a sweet release of tension. I had witnessed a miracle.

My knee pain had not subsided, but was a little better than earlier in the morning. It continued to bother me, and massage, Ace bandages and anti-inflammatory medicines were not helpful. I hoped God would intervene and heal my knee. But, why would He do that? Was I so special? I do all the wrong things—I lie, I cheat, I'm dishonest, I'm jealous, and I'm not charitable enough. On the other hand, I'm not such a bad person. I've done some good deeds too. I've helped the sick, I go to the temple often, and I even volunteer there. I also take care of my family.

Do I really think I deserve a break? Have I been a good student, following Lord's covenants? I kept on talking to myself, trying to plead a case in my mind as if God was judging me for my virtues, which were paltry at its best.

Finally I decided to seek the expertise of my orthopedic colleague.

Chapter 8

OFFICE VISIT—DR. KAPLAN

It was time to get my knee examined again. Dr. Walter, who had examined my knee ten years ago, had retired. Dr. Kaplan had joined that practice a few years later and had matured into a reputable orthopedic surgeon in the same practice. I called and talked to him about the situation with my knee. He said, "Raj, come on over and let me examine your knee, take X-rays and see what is going on."

I scheduled my visit with him the following day and walked down the hall into their office. A majestic aquarium greeted me as I stepped into the large waiting room—a floor to ceiling, ten feet wide and two feet deep body of water. Multicolored fish swimming in their own splendor against the deep blue background captivated me and provided comfort. The chairs, carpet and the wall coverings were perfectly matched in light and dark blue contrast. I picked up a magazine and sat down, but kept admiring the aquarium. Water always soothes me. It can be a small aquarium or a huge body of water, like an ocean, but it always has a calming effect.

After a short wait the nurse called my name, and I followed her inside to the examination room.

"How are you Dr. Bhushan? I'm Gail. What brings you here?"

"My left knee has been painful for the past two days."

"Did you injure your knee?"

"No. I had gone out for a walk when it started to hurt."

"Have you taken any medications to relieve the pain?"

"Yes, I have been taking Motrin for the past two days, but it didn't help."

"Do you take any medicines on a regular basis?"

"No, I don't."

"Do you have any drug allergies?"

"No."

She took my blood pressure and pulse, then said, "Dr. Kaplan will be in shortly" and left the exam room.

Sitting in the exam room, I vividly remembered Dr. Walter's prophetic comment from ten years ago: 'You'll need surgery sometime in the future.' This time I knew I had a bigger problem.

Dr. Kaplan came in a few minutes later. He's a fine-looking man in his forties, with salt and pepper straight hair and a distinguished upright posture. With my file in his hand and a friendly smile he asked, "Hey Raj, What is going on?"

"Tom, my left knee is hurting. I had gone out for a walk, and halfway through the walk, it suddenly started to ache. The pain seems to be in the back and inner side and at times I felt I could not fully bend my knee." I narrated Dr. Walter's findings from ten years ago when I had injured my knee playing basketball with my son.

"Did you feel the knee was going to give out on you?"

"No. It wasn't that."

"Let me examine your knee," he said. He twisted and turned it and checked the range of motion, as well as the capacity for strength and weight bearing. One particular maneuver caused a sharp pain in the inner aspect, deep inside my knee. When I winced in pain, he looked at me. "I am sorry, I didn't mean to hurt you, but it definitely looks like a torn medial meniscus."

The knee joint has two kidney shaped structures called Menisci on either side of the knee joint. The Medial is on the inner side of the knee where as the

Lateral is on the outside. They are thick on the outside, closer to the surface near the skin and gradually become thinner inside, between the bones. They are spongy and act as shock absorbers between the femur and the tibia, the thigh and the calf, and are prone to wear and tear with physical activity and age.

"Are you sure, Tom?"

"I'm almost certain it's a torn meniscus. Let me write you a prescription for an MRI scan. It will confirm my clinical evaluation. You'll need Arthroscopic repair for this. Come back and see me after the MRI."

The MRI scan was scheduled for the same day, across the street in the other medical office building. The scan took about thirty minutes. I have been in this radiology center many times, looking at the scans of my patients with the radiologists. Afterwards, the nurse took me into the senior Radiologist's office for the review of the scan of my knee. The technology of MRI scanning had evolved significantly since my previous scan ten years ago. The resolution of the scanner was superb and the image quality was much more detailed. In the past decade, physicists, scientists and mathematicians have been able to provide us with new gadgetry and tools to look inside the human body without invading the tissues. In this new digital age, the scan was available to review in less than thirty minutes.

Dr. Murphy, Chief of Radiology looked at the scan and said, "Raj, you have a large complex tear of medial meniscus of the left knee. I think it will require arthroscopic repair." I wondered for a moment if he was sure. *He's a Radiologist. What does he know about surgery and knee joints? Is he even reading my MRI scan?* I looked at the name on the corner of the MRI films, and sure enough they were mine. *Oh boy, here comes the surgery.* I thanked Dr. Murphy for taking the time to show me the MRI scan and quietly walked out of their office. I was hoping that Dr. Kaplan would say that it wasn't too bad, that physical therapy and rest would fix the problem. But I had seen the MRI scan with my own two eyes and the tear was much worse than the injury the MRI showed ten years ago. I knew surgery was the only way to deal with this torn meniscus. Deep in my thoughts, I carried the jacket containing the films to Dr. Kaplan's office.

Dr. Kaplan looked at the scan and suggested I get the knee fixed. I had come to terms with the decision even before Dr. Kaplan mentioned it. Procrastination was not going to heal the damaged knee, so I decided to schedule the surgery as soon as possible.

"Let's schedule surgery and get you a date," he said.

He started explaining the procedure, the possible complications and the recovery. He told me that the procedure usually takes about an hour. I would go home the same day, and I would be back at work within a week. We spent the next few minutes talking about our families and the busy schedules. He wished me well and I thanked him for his time and parted.

I stopped by my office on the way back to tell my office manager Jackie about my upcoming surgery, and to rearrange the office schedule.

"Don't worry, Dr. B." she said, "You take care of you. Your knee has been hurting for some time. I'll take care of things here at the office."

I came home and discussed everything with Manju and Mom. They both felt uncomfortable with the idea of an operation.

"Is surgery the only way to relieve the pain in your knee?" Manju asked.

"Yes. I've seen the MRI scan and there is a bad tear."

"Do you want to wait and try rest, physical therapy and massage?"

"No. The tear is large in the meniscus and I don't think it will heal by itself. Surgery is the only option."

"Well, you're the doctor and you know best. Have you scheduled the surgery yet?"

"Yes. My surgery is scheduled for next Tuesday morning, before Thanksgiving Day."

Chapter 9

DEVELOPMENT OF FAITH

My visits to the local Hindu temple were limited to special events. Representing the congregation as an officer and a trustee was more important to me in the old days than the real faith. Sitting in the temple, my mind was usually occupied with other people and what they were doing. My mind would wander in all directions during services, and it was rarely if ever focused on God, His blessings or my faith. I wanted to be recognized by everybody, including the priest, other trustees and officers of the board for my contribution to the cause. Focusing on others' shortcomings became the main distraction of my visits to the temple. Of course this internal commotion made me feel guilty. *Am I here to impress people or is my visit to this temple for God's purpose?* I felt as though I were cheating

God and making a fool of myself. *Do I deserve to be here in this sanctuary of God? Is this temple really a place of worship? I see people gossiping and chit-chatting.* For a few minutes I would settle down and then my mind would drift yet again.

Maybe I'll bribe God with a little cash donation and He will do all the right things, really big things for me—didn't this make sense? For a small contribution a much larger return. This was how I negotiated with God.

Hinduism is a way of life. The philosophy believes in reincarnation based on the theory of '*Karma*', where the consequences of our actions are either immediate, intermediate or in the next three cycles of birth and death, according to the Vedic (Holy Scripture) principles. It is extremely difficult to understand when a particular individual, family or society is doing all the wrong things and yet remains prosperous and happy—at least that is what appears on the outside. *Karma* ultimately catches up with everyone, but to witness this requires patience.

Hinduism was often trapped in the ritualistic aspect of the religion. Illiteracy and ignorance played a major role in practice of ritualizing. There are quite a few Gods and Goddesses, and in different parts of the country, north to south, east to west, people have beliefs in their favorite God. The religious system is vast and fragmented at its best, but the core values remain: forgiveness, tolerance, self-control and non-violence.

I grew up in the environment of rituals. What is a ritual? It is a set form of rites in a religion, an offering to God for something in return. It is always associated with a net gain, a sort of negotiation with God. But as I grew older, I felt that for a small gratification of material things, I sacrificed a much larger entity—God's love, eternal peace and happiness. I didn't understand my real purpose, so the pursuit of small future gains became the primary objective of my visits to the temple. The offerings, contributions and donations were always tied to something in return. God's love and my faith were not any of my concern as long as my material desires were promptly fulfilled. Uncomfortable with my thoughts as I sat in the center of the prayer hall, I was scared to look at the deities. I felt that even if I mustered enough courage to look at one of them, the blood-shot eyes of the deity Lord Rama would scream at me, *Hey you, you sitting in the center of this prayer hall, you phony, what are you doing here?*

So I shied away from making any eye contact. I feared the wrath of God coming straight out of that marble structure towards me. I stayed quiet, doing my ritualistic offering and walking away lest the fury unfold at any moment.

I couldn't concentrate at all. I was more interested in the social drama around me. Driving back home, I wondered what I gained from visiting the temple. Was it of any benefit or was I mocking religion by mimicking a sanctimonious appearance? On rare occasions, I did connect with the Almighty. I cursed myself during those moments not for the peace it gave me, but for the paucity of the peace. I knew the war was not over but there was hope. The very fear of wrong thoughts provoked a desire to correct my course, and bit-by-bit this desire propelled me in the right direction.

During the course of a number of years, I had many patients come into the office and talk about God and faith. I would listen to them and agree with them in that moment, but the effects of those conversations were short lived. External forces of daily life would overpower the effect and dilute faith again. I had my share of troubles and faith never took a strong hold in the deepest part of me.

Chapter 10

STRUGGLES

On November 18, 1984, we welcomed our second son Sonny into the world. Five hours into the labor, the fetal heartbeat suddenly dropped to sixty, and I knew a normal heartbeat should be one hundred forty. The obstetrician rushed in, obviously concerned about the fetal heart rate. Frozen, I stood in the delivery room as I watched the baby's head emerge, ashen gray in color, followed by the neck with the umbilical cord wrapped around it. The baby was bluish in color initially, then slowly turned pink as the cord was untangled. The weak shrill confirmed that the baby was alive, and I breathed a sigh of relief.

But because of my medical background, I knew there might be something wrong with my son. I had seen the drop in his heart rate, I had seen the cord around his neck, and I had watched the blue lifeless baby slowly come to life with a rather weak shrill and not the strong cry of a normal new born. I carried the baby in my arms as if everything was well and good, but I knew some problems lay ahead for us. I didn't want to burden Manju with all the details yet. For now, in the labor and delivery, the mother was happy to learn the baby was alive and well.

Sonny was born with deformed feet. He had a severe case of Cerebral Palsy and had seizures from birth. This condition caused paralysis of his left side. By the time he was three months old I noticed he was not focusing on any object, and I immediately set up an appointment with a pediatric eye specialist. I will never forget that day. Manju accompanied me with our helpless baby to the ophthalmologist's office. Manju stayed in the reception area while I took our son in the exam room. Dr. Frank spent a lot of time examining him, doing all sorts of tests.

He finished the exam, paused for a moment, looked at me, came close and put his hand on my shoulder. "Dr. B, your son will never be able to see."

His words sent a shocking chill through my spine.

"His retina is not developed. I am sorry," he continued. "Your son is blind."

My heart stopped with a hard thump in my chest. I didn't know what to do. Cry? Scream at the top of my voice? Sit down, stand up or run? *What will I tell Manju? She won't understand. She'll be devastated. Can she bear it? Oh God! What should I do? Please help me God.* I stood there for several minutes, although it seemed like an eternity. I held my little son in my arms and kissed him and slowly walked out of the exam room, smiling and talking to him as if nothing had happened. I completely locked up my emotions that day so that my poor wife would not be heart broken. I came out in the reception area where she was eagerly waiting for me. "What did the doctor say? Is Sonny alright?"

I looked at her and said, "Yes. But he needs further test at Johns Hopkins Hospital."

She was not satisfied and asked, "Is his vision and eyesight normal?"

"There is some problem but we are not sure. Dr. Frank has recommended special tests." Internally I was overwhelmed. I knew what type of challenges lay ahead. Putting a cheerful face on for Manju was not easy, but I felt I had no choice. Manju was already going through so much. I felt lonely. Up until now my faith had been no more than a convenience. When things went my way, my faith was there, but when they didn't, watch out. I'm ashamed to say that I only wanted faith on my terms, on my turf. I began to curse God. *Why me? Why has this child come into our family? Why are you doing this to us? You have not been fair to me. You have ignored my family and me. I hate you for what you have done.*

The cursing continued for a few minutes until fear of what else could happen strangled my rage, and I stopped abusing God. But what could I do? I was not ready to accept this as God's Will. No amount of reasoning would provide comfort. Drained, I asked for help from the same entity I cursed, feeling ashamed of my previous abuse. Completely helpless, we left the doctor's office and drove back home.

Dr. Martin, a well-known pediatric ophthalmologist at The Wilmer Eye Institute at Johns Hopkins, later evaluated Sonny. After multiple visits and numerous tests, it was concluded that Sonny was blind. His retina suffered damage sometime during the pregnancy.

Sonny lived in a vegetative state for nineteen years before passing away. There were many times I would sit in my own private moments and quarrel with God, blame Him for everything, argue with Him, and sometimes even scream at Him at the top of my voice. It cracked me emotionally, and tore me to pieces until I would come to my senses and tell myself, 'I can't blame God for all this. How can I? God has provided for my family and me in many other ways.'

Sonny never spoke a word and needed round-the-clock attention. By the end of his life, he needed two adults to lift him and sometimes help was not easy to find. Manju and I talked about placing him in a nursing home or an institution, but these conversations always ended in our acceptance of God's Will. We feel blessed that we kept him at home and he passed away peacefully in our presence.

My faith fluctuated on several occasions. I am only human. But every year that passed by, my faith became stronger until I felt His divine presence in my life more than ever. Now my faith was going to be tested again.

Chapter 11

REGISTRATION

Tuesday morning, the day of the surgery, I woke up at seven a.m. I hadn't slept well because I couldn't stop worrying about the surgery. As soon as I opened my eyes, the realization hit me that today was not a day for business as usual. *Today is the day of my surgery.* I got up and brushed my teeth, did my morning rituals, took a hot bath, dressed and came into the kitchen for breakfast. *Oh, I can't eat today.* I have to fast for the surgery. I didn't realize how programmed I'd been for all these years to eat breakfast before heading to work, but not today. Manju was already dressed and waiting for me in the kitchen. She had been keenly watching me all morning. We had very little conversation, as we both seem to be preoccupied with the thought of the trip to the hospital. I was terrified and anxious with the thought of surgery. I just didn't want anyone to know about it. I had to show a strong facade.

"Are you ready?" Manju asked.

"Yes." I said. "I guess I have no choice."

"Are you scared?"

"No. Not really. I'm fine." Soon enough though, I felt butterflies in my stomach, and my heart started racing.

"I've put a few things together in a bag in case you stay longer in the hospital."

"You're right." I replied, "You never know."

Mom came over and wished me well. "Please let me know once you're out of the operating room."

"Mom, I'll call you. Please don't worry" Manju replied.

I sat quietly in the car, on the passenger side. I didn't want to go to the hospital. Sadness, depression and fear occupied my mind. We pulled out of the garage and headed towards the Dulles Toll Road between Washington DC and Dulles Airport. It's a busy eight-lane highway. Reston Hospital is located right off Fairfax County parkway two blocks from the Dulles Toll road. I wanted to get my mind off the upcoming surgery, so I focused on the different cars on the road and the passing scenery. But the internal commotion was too strong to let me forget where we were going. As we got closer to the hospital, I became a nervous wreck. I tried my best to act like a strong, healthy man, but my nerves were out of control. I would tell myself to calm down and take a deep breath, everything would be fine, but the inner pep-talk wasn't helping. The fierce fight within me continued as we made a left turn into the hospital campus.

Reston hospital was built in 1987 and subsequently expanded into a much larger facility three years ago. The cluster of four tan brick buildings came into view; five stories each, housing the hospital and the medical offices. *We're here now, Dr. B. Get hold of yourself.* The inner roads connecting the buildings and the parking garages are well maintained and landscaped with trees on both sides. We came to the front entrance of the building named The Pavilion. This building houses the same day surgery on the main level, and my office is on the fourth floor.

Manju pulled the car in front of the canopied entrance, and the valet came forward to get the keys to park the car. The valet service is provided as courtesy to patients and their families, a service that was started while the parking garage was being built in the late 1990's. I had never used this valet service before, and it felt odd asking the valet to park our car. The three valets at the entrance; dressed in navy overalls, were so involved in exchange of car keys that they were not concerned with who was coming or leaving the hospital. We collected the ticket from the valet to go in to the hospital. My whole body and especially my legs felt weak and I lacked the energy to get up. My brain commanded me to get out of the car and walk into the hospital, but the strong grip of anxiety would not loosen its hold. I felt numb. *Let me stay in the car a few more minutes. Do I have to go in? Is the surgery necessary? Yes,* I told myself, *I have seen the MRI scan; it's not going to get better by itself. There is no other option. Get up and move.* Manju was observing all this but didn't say anything. She probably had the same tug-of-war going on in her mind. I got out of the car and entered the Pavilion through the automatic double doors.

To the right of the lobby the registration desk loomed before us. I walked into the waiting area for out-patient surgery, the first of the many stops before surgery. I sat down and looked around, observed things I never paid attention to before. The oblong registration desk encroached into the hallway about two feet. It was fairly small area behind the desk, barely enough for two chairs. The entrance to this area was through the Registration office located behind it. The patient waiting area had fifteen chairs, light blue in color, matching the wall covering and the carpet. I've walked these hallways and passed this area hundreds of times since the hospital opened in 1987 and yet this landscape was all taken for granted. Today, as I sat with Manju, I noticed the smoke detectors, sprinkler heads and air vents. There were other patients and family members in the waiting area. Everyone was busy checking papers, insurance cards and health related issues. Some of them were just sitting there deep in their own thoughts.

Within a few minutes my name was called and I followed the clerk to the registration office. She directed me to one of the small cubicles and asked me to sit down. She took my insurance information and informed me of my obligation to pay for services not covered by the insurance. It felt odd to hear the words, 'my obligation to pay for services.' For many years I've been providing services, giving my time, and often going out of my way to attend the health care needs of others without any concern for payment for my services. I felt almost insulted, as if she were saying *Look out, we'll punish you if you don't meet your obligation.* Scolding me in advance for something I would never do.

I knew it wasn't her fault. She was just following the protocol. Keeping her eyes on the big computer monitor, she confirmed my address, phone number and emergency contact numbers. She put a plastic bracelet on my wrist with my name and patient number. It felt strange to have a bracelet with a number on my wrist, to be a numbered individual, in an institution. I felt as if I were in jail, in an enclosed structure called the hospital for the crime of having a damaged knee, to be punished by anesthesia and surgery. *Isn't it funny to be in this position,* I thought to myself. *No! This is not funny. What am I doing here? I don't want to be here. I don't want to register. I don't want to be a patient. What have I gotten myself into? I should have listened to Manju all these years and forgotten about my obsession with jogging. If I had, I wouldn't be in this predicament.'*

As I rose to go back to the waiting area, I heard somebody call "Hey! Dr. B; what are you doing here?" A dear patient of mine was registering in the next cubicle for a colonoscopy.

"I have a torn meniscus in my knee that needs arthroscopic surgery. I'll have the surgery this morning."

"Those suckers hurt. I had one done a few years ago," he said. We wished each other well and parted.

Suddenly it dawned on me that I was 'Patient Bhushan' for the day. I was on the other side.

Chapter 12

PRE≈SURGERY

The hallway from the registration area led to a much larger surgical waiting area. The carpeted hallway had light blue and taupe color carpet with a zigzag pattern with matching wallpaper. There were forty-six chairs, dividing the area into smaller sections. The taupe end tables held all sorts of newspapers and magazines. I wondered how many people waiting there really read them, or if they were too wrapped up in the fear and anxiety associated with illness. The waiting area buzzed with hospital employees, patients and their families. The red vinyl chairs showed wear and tear from heavy usage. The coffee maker with two pots of coffee was placed on a counter in one corner along with the condiments, next to the water fountain. Three gigantic vending machines occupied the remaining wall of the waiting area. On the opposite side sat the information desk, staffed by a volunteer to answer any questions and issues for the waiting families.

Two wall-mounted TV's were showing "The Price is Right". Bob Barker had been hosting this show for as long as I can remember. I sat there with Manju, waiting for my name to be called, lost in my own thoughts, oblivious to the surroundings and other times all too aware of what was happening around me. If I ran away, what would every body say? I couldn't sit still. I was going nuts.

I wanted to go over to the water fountain, but I wasn't thirsty. *Maybe I could go to the vending machine for some munchies, but I'm not hungry; and I can't eat or drink anything anyway before surgery.* The TV show wasn't appealing anymore; the magazines were boring. My lips were dry, my tongue parched, and I couldn't swallow. *What is going on? Am I having a panic attack? Control your emotions, what will your wife think? Worse, what will all these patients and their families sitting in this waiting room think? You're a doctor, a well-known doctor in this hospital. Take a deep breath and calm down.* I started thinking of my patients who had gone through surgery and felt sorry for them. *I'll make sure I reassure everyone from here on.* I scold my self,' For a brief moment, I calmed down and then the panic began to build all over again.

My breathing came and went in short gasps, and the churning inside become unstoppable. My fertile mind visualized the operating room, and how I'd feel under anesthesia. *What if I become paralyzed and nobody there knows about it in time? What if I suffer a stroke during the procedure and am unable to speak or swallow? Or worse, I become disabled and confined to a wheel chair? If I can't swallow, they'll have to put a feeding tube into my stomach, but I don't want to live that way. I don't want to die either. Oh God, what is happening to me? Why don't You do anything? Oh God, Please help me.* My eyes filled with tears, and I looked around to see if anybody noticed. *'Dr. B, what are you doing. You should be ashamed of yourself. Stop being an emotional wreck. You're making a fool of yourself. Please God, make the clock run faster so that it's all finished and I can leave this hospital.*

I continued talking to myself. *Dr. B, you have always talked about God, faith and trust in the Almighty. What has happened to you? Do you doubt God's plans? Whatever the plan is, it will be right one for you. You just have to put all your faith in the supreme Power and go along for this ride. You cannot fall apart. You have to put your faith to the test now. This is the time.* I quietly sit down for a moment.

Chapter 13

DILEMMA

The waiting room was full of activity. Everybody was preoccupied with his or her families. I started a conversation with Manju about an unrelated topic, just to get my mind off the surgery. Briefly, I started to feel better. I looked around at the two children, about four and six years of age, playing with a little video game they had brought from home. They were so absorbed in that little gadget, totally oblivious to the problems of the other patients in the room. Everybody sitting around me had an expression of concern, except for these two boys. At that age, their whole world was that video game.

My office assistant Janet stopped by and wished me well. To my anxious ears, her sincere 'all the best' sounded suspicious, and I wondered for a moment why she wished me well. Was this a final good bye? Did she know something I didn't? *I may not come out of surgery alive.* My mortality suddenly seemed an imminent reality; the final deal; the last chapter in the book of my life. *People die everyday in hospitals. I am not immune. I'm a patient today, just like every one else. What will happen to my family, Manju, my mother, my son and his wife, my brother, my friends, my practice, my patients?*

Manju will be left alone. She loves me so much. Emotionally, it will be very difficult for her, but she is a strong person. Should I tell her what to do if I am gone? My poor wife, what will she do? I have enough Life Insurance. She has a decent job. Financially, she will be able to manage. She will be all right. I can't talk to her about all this. She has her family and friends for support and she believes in God. She will be able to overcome the loss, but I think she will miss me a lot. We have had our share of arguments, but we have had a close and loving relationship for several years. Let me at least tell her how much I love her and how much I appreciate her being there for me before I go in for surgery.

I am just having an arthroscopic knee surgery. Come on, Dr. B, you're stressing yourself for such a minor procedure. Calm down. Rest your brain. Everything will be fine.

Manju put her hand on my arm, shaking me a bit, interrupting my thoughts, "You have been sitting here, so deep in your thoughts for the past few minutes that I didn't have the heart to disturb you. What's going on?"

"Oh! It's nothing. I just want you to know I love you. Thanks for being here for me."

"I love you too. You know I am always here for you. Where else would I be? Now tell me what is bothering you."

"It's nothing" I replied, "I'm just anxious about what will happen."

"I know. So am I. Things will be fine. Have faith."

"Patient Bhushan," I heard someone call. Ever since I graduated from medical school in 1974, I've been called Dr. Bhushan. My brain has been programmed to respond to only that name, and at first the name "Patient Bhushan" didn't register.

"What time is it?" I asked Manju.

"Eleven. They called your name. Did you hear it?"

"Yes! I heard it. I guess it's time for me to go."

I don't want to be a patient. 'Patients' are a different breed. They suffer in pain and get needle sticks, infected wounds and blood clots. I knew that most of them got better, but some of them got into real trouble with all sorts of complications, and a small percentage of them never made it. *I hope I am not one of them. I am scared, really scared. What is going to happen? Why do I have to go with this operating room technician now? Please help me God. Please help me.* I felt like crying, but I had to smile and show my wife that everything was fine. *Dr. B, relax. Calm down. You're already becoming the worst patient and you haven't had anything done yet.*

I quietly got up and walked over to where the OR Tech was standing and said, "Hi, I'm Patient Bhushan."

The operating Room Technician looked at me in surprise smiled and said with enthusiasm, "Hey Dr. B, I didn't know this was you." I have seen this O R Tech in the hallways for many years. I didn't know his name, but we always shared a passing greeting. He took me in the pre-op holding area, checked my temperature, blood pressure, pulse, and weight, and gave me a hospital gown and asked me to lie down on the stretcher. As I looked around at other patients, nurses and technicians I felt a need to talk to them, listen to their problems and share my worries with them.

In the middle of all these varied thoughts, a nurse walked in and introduced herself. "Mr. Bhushan, good morning. I'm Linda, your nurse here in the pre-op." *Who am I today, Mr. Bhushan, Dr. Bhushan or Patient Bhushan? My designation is changing every few minutes.* This nurse didn't know I was a practicing physician in the hospital, and I didn't mention it to her. I wanted to be treated just like any other patient.

She consulted my chart. "You're here for arthroscopy on your left knee."

"Yes. I have a torn meniscus."

She looked at me sitting on the gurney still wearing the clothes I came to the hospital in and said, "You need to change into that gown."

"Do I need to take my undergarments off too?"

"Yes, everything off. I'll step out to give you some privacy."

I smiled and felt stupid. I see patients' everyday with their clothes off, when they're in my office for physical exams. I changed, lay down on the gurney and stared at the ceiling lights and the drapes around the cubicle.

She returned in a couple of minutes and continued her pleasant conversation.

"How did you tear the meniscus?" she asked, making small talk with me while going about doing her work.

"I was playing basketball with my son."

"I'm going to hook you up to a monitor to check your vital signs." She asked about my past health history, family health history, medications, allergies, and informed me that she would start an IV. Cleaning the top part of my hand with alcohol and an antiseptic solution, she introduced the needle and attached the intravenous tubing to it. It hurt a little bit, but it wasn't too bad. I figured this would be nothing compared to the pain after the surgery. I could imagine the plight of patients who lived with the need for IV access and had their blood drawn multiple times a day. I admired their courage.

She completed securing the IV and asked, "Did it hurt?"

"No, not really, just a little bit."

"I'm sorry if I hurt you. I'll put an additional tape on it so that we don't lose it during transport. Is this your first surgery?"

"Yes, this is the first time, and I am nervous about the whole process."

With a reassuring smile, she patted my arm and said, "Please let me know if you need anything. We're here to help you."

"Thank you. I will." Her reassurance was soothing and it restored my confidence, at least for the moment.

"The Anesthesiologist will be in to talk to you shortly and I'll be back to check on you in a few minutes," she said, and left.

This was the first step to the operating room. At least she was concerned about my wellbeing and explained to me what was going to happen next. *It helps a lot when people around you care.*

The pre-op holding area was divided into small cubicles about seven foot wide and ten foot deep, separated by drapes. It had an L shaped nursing station, which could monitor all the eight cubicles. I lay there in a small-enclosed area no different than the patient in the cubicle next to me, an ordinary human being at the mercy of technicians, nurses and anesthesiologists.

Dr. Brown from the anesthesia walked in asked, "Hey, Dr. B, How are you doing?" Dr. Brown, a bright looking young doctor, had joined the anesthesia staff at the hospital two years ago. "Dr. B, do you have any preference for anesthesia? We can go either way, general or spinal."

"You're the expert." I replied. "Will you please explain to me the pros and cons of each?"

"Sure. With the spinal anesthesia, we'll give you a local anesthetic with a tiny needle to make the area numb, then introduce a long needle in your lower back, usually between lumbar first and second vertebra into the sac covering the spinal cord." This sac contains cerebrospinal fluid, which bathes the brain and continuously flows between the brain and the spinal cord.

"With the spinal anesthesia, you'll be awake throughout the surgery, but you won't feel anything. You'll have numbness and weakness in the legs for up to three hours," he said, "and some times you can have urinary retention, particularly in men over the age of fifty." He paused, looked at me and waited for a response.

I listened to him carefully. My mind analyzed the information and suddenly it hit me: *Oh, my God! I am past fifty. Where have all the years gone? Fifty two years old—Dr. B, you're getting old! Urinary retention is no fun. They will have to insert a Foley catheter if I am not able to go on my own. Ouch!*

I started having tingling sensations in my privates. *No! No way am I going to have someone insert a tube in me. Are you crazy, Dr. B? How many Foley Catheterizations have you ordered as a practicing physician? Do you realize the fear, anxiety and discomfort it causes to the patients? What am*

I afraid of? A whirlwind of emotions started to play havoc with me.

Dr. Brown was still talking and I had to force my thoughts aside and listen to him, "With the spinal anesthesia there could be nerve damage in the spinal cord and potential weakness and/or paralysis of the legs."

My knee is the reason for my visit to the hospital, and I may develop nerve damage from the spinal anesthesia and become paralyzed. What am I doing? I asked him about general anesthesia.

"Well, you'll be completely sedated," he said. "No urinary retention, and there are no issues with nerve damage, but, there are other potential complications, like hoarseness of voice with tracheal intubations, not to mention cardiovascular complications, which are rare." He paused. "It is your choice."

At that moment, Dr. Horowitz, the senior Anesthesiologist walked in. I had known Dr. Horowitz for many years and had a lot of respect for him. He listened to the discussion about spinal vs. general anesthesia and said, "Dr. B, it's your choice. We can do either one."

"Dr. Horowitz, What would you do if you were getting operated?"

He looked straight into my eyes and said, "General anesthesia is the way to go, Dr. B."

I tapped into the deepest voice inside me and the direction came to me very quickly about having general anesthesia. "I think you're right. That's what I will have. Thanks for your input."

I could understand the mental anguish patients felt when they had to make the decision about anesthesia or surgery. I'd been a practicing doctor for twenty five years and I couldn't decide what type of anesthesia to have for a routine arthroscopy. What about all those patients who have to make these decisions everyday? *God bless them.* Because of this experience, I realized what my patents went through to have surgery in a hospital. It was frightening. I felt at ease once the decision was made about the type of anesthesia, though the fear of complication still loomed in the background.

Dr. Brown said, "You have to sign the consent form for anesthesia." I reviewed the consent form for general anesthesia and signed at the bottom of the page. It felt as if I were signing my life away.

"Dr. B, we'll see you in the operating room in a few minutes. You're going to be completely sedated and unconscious very soon." As I listened to Dr. Brown, the chain reaction of fear started again. I pictured myself lying on the operating table, completely unconscious, a breathing tube inserted through my nostril, into my airway, the ventilator pumping oxygen and anesthesia into my lungs every few seconds. IV tubing attached to a bag of saline infused my vein while the monitor displayed my vital signs. What if more than the usual amount of anesthetic went in? What if the anesthesiologist wasn't careful about monitoring the medicines and vital signs? Things could go wrong. What if they weren't able to reverse the effect of the anesthesia? I'd be in medication-induced coma—a state of suspended animation. The team of doctors would struggle to wake me up, but to no

THE WIDE OPEN DOOR

avail. That would be horrible. Manju would be waiting outside, wondering what was going on. *Run, Dr. B, run. You don't want to go through this. This is scary. I can live with this pain in my knee. I don't have to be operated on today. I can wait a month, a year or a lifetime. May be it will heal by itself.*

Run!

Chapter 14

CONTAINER OF LOVE

It seems to be extremely difficult for doctors, engineers' mathematicians and the erudite elite to believe in God. They want to have a scientific explanation for faith. There has to be a theory, a formulation or a calculation that adds up to faith. Like $a + b + c - d = faith$.

The very definition of faith defies scientific logic. Faith is trust or confidence in the Power that is beyond us. It develops over time. In our lives, so many things happen on a daily basis, some in our favor and some against our will. We accept them and move on. There are many things, big or small, over which we have no control. We are pushed into a corner, we feel trapped and helpless, but when things fall back into place with no plausible explanation, we wonder *how this is possible?* Faith is the belief in that energy which is beyond us, which solves the puzzle without our intervention.

Recently, there was a service at the local Hindu temple, and we were asked by the priest to help with the services. Before the event, I pulled a muscle in my groin while doing leg lifts. My orthopedist prescribed therapeutic exercises, which I did three times a week, but somehow, the relief was minimal, and the day of the service was approaching fast.

During the service I had to sit on the floor, in a half lotus—Indian position, with the priest for two hours to read the Holy book—*Ramayan*. The services started at eleven-thirty in the morning. For the first ten minutes, it was uncomfortable to sit in that position, but my mind was fully occupied in reciting God's word over and over to the congregation. The more I read, the better I felt. After the services, I rose to my feet and realized that my muscle strain had completely vanished. Was I surprised or shocked? Not really. My faith took another leap.

After the sermon, lunch was provided to the congregation. The priest came over and whispered into my ear, "Looks like we have over two hundred people today. How much food did you order?" I turned around to see the hall was packed. Typically we have around one hundred people who come for the services, and I had requested lunch for a hundred and fifty from the caterer. I stood there in the prayer hall; my breath caught in my throat, convinced that we would run out of food. I swallowed a couple times before I could say,

"We are in the house of worship. The Lord will help us out" and walked down the steps to the dining hall. *Dear Lord, this is your temple, this is your congregation, and this is your food. I have faith. You take over. Please feed everybody, like you always do.*

I saw a long line of congregation members; six volunteers served them lunch. The volunteers looked anxious. I went over to the kitchen and asked the caterer, "How much food is left?" He said, "Plenty of food. Not to worry."

That day, people kept coming, the volunteers kept serving and the Lord kept providing more. I stood there, praying: *Dear Almighty God, I will not eat today until every one is fed through your Grace.* The flow of people and the serving of food went on for an hour. There was no one left unfed. After the line was gone, the volunteers finally took their lunch. I stood there in awe looking at the food table. By the end over two hundred and fifty people had been served, and yet there was enough left to feed at least ten more. My hunger had completely vanished. I felt satisfied and at peace. Manju, Alex and Rita came over and asked me to get my plate of food so we could sit down together and eat. As I put bread on my plate I thanked God:. *Dear Lord, you left so much food for me. My heart is filled with gratitude. You know I love you so much. Please forgive me when I falter or when my faith is shaken.*

My mother is a devout Hindu, and I was raised as a Hindu. Every Tuesday morning she started her day with a visit to the local temple. The rest of the week, she would read the holy book *Ramayan* early in the morning before starting her day. I would listen to her recite it to me in my earlier years, and started reading it myself before I turned ten. Once a year, during the summer vacation, we organized the reading of the holy book continuously over a span of twenty-four hours. In this way I grew up in an atmosphere of faith and belief in Almighty God. I enjoyed reading the Holy book, going to the temple and listening to God's word through local priests. In spite of all this, however, I poorly understood the real meaning of faith.

As a little boy, I couldn't bear to see the poor, the sick or the hungry. I would give my daily allowance to anyone I saw who was poor or had very little to eat. Often, my parents scolded me for doing so. They were worried someone might abduct me because they thought we had lots of money.

During tough times, family tragedies, happy occasions, God was always in my thoughts. It seemed He was my best friend. I always talked to God. As a child, I would ask Him to help me get good grades in school, and sometimes I would even ask Him to do my homework because I was too busy playing. I would seek His help to get out of trouble. Once as a teenager, I smoked a cigarette and became nauseous and light headed. I was scared that my parents were going to find out and I would be grounded. I begged God to forgive me and promised God I would never smoke again if He got me out of trouble this time. That was the first and last time I smoked a cigarette.

I have always asked for His love and forgiveness. At times, I was busy and forgot Him, but somehow He always came back in my life stronger than ever.

I always knew God existed somewhere out there, and I always asked for things from Him, like a big brother, but I never really understood the meaning of faith.

Chapter 15

CRUTCHES

I lay on the stretcher, lost in my thoughts until the orthopedic technician came in and introduced himself as John. He must have been in his late thirties, a shade under six feet tall with straight black hair, neatly combed away from his face. "Hi Dr. B, I'm here to talk to you about your crutches. How tall are you?"

"Five feet six," I replied.

"I'll bring the crutches for your frame." A few minutes later, he was back with a pair of crutches and demonstrated how to use them. Support your legs, pressure on the armpits; put the good leg this way and the operated leg that way. I kept listening to him carefully to understand exactly how to use this new contraption.

He finished his presentation in about ten minutes and asked, "Do you understand how to use these?"

"I guess I will have to learn. I've never used these before." *Thank God,* I thought.

"It is not difficult. You'll need them for three to five days, sometimes up to a week or more. Let me know if you have any questions."

Anxiety triggered another conversation with God. I was looking at the crutches and thought to myself *Who is the best supporter of human body? It is no one other than Almighty God. Where did this physical strength come from? It is no one other than Dear Lord. When I was a baby and stood for the first time, who supported me? It was no one other than God. He has supported me from the day I was born. Who was I before I was born? I was a particle of energy, invisible, nameless and placeless flowing energy. That energy was there then and is here now, so why am I worried? Is my faith not strong enough to overcome this obstacle? Why am I shaky? No! I have full faith. Let the crutches stay here. I don't think I will need them. I know where my support will come from.*

I asked Manju to put the crutches under my stretcher to follow the protocol, so every one would be happy. My dear wife looked at the crutches and then at me as if I were going to be disabled. "Do you understand how to use these things?"

"No! Not really. But I've seen people walk with them. The orthopedic tech just explained it. It shouldn't be difficult. I will manage"

She smiled and said, "How will you manage? You're such a baby. Let me see." She examined the crutches, but I could see some degree of fear and anxiety on her face. I know she was trying to act tough, but her eyes filled with tears. "Don't worry, I will help you" she said, probably more to convince herself than me. She was never at ease in hospitals, but was trying to cheer me up.

A short while later I had the urge to use the restroom. As I walked down the hallway, one of my colleagues saw me in a hospital gown, dragging an IV pole. He was taken aback. "Dr. B, are you having surgery? Are you alright?"

"Yes, I am having surgery for a torn meniscus in my knee. I injured it playing basketball with my son."

"I had a torn ligament in my knee several years back from playing racket ball. It took me three months to fully recover. I was on crutches and painkillers for a while. It was no fun. Who is operating on you?"

"Dr. Kaplan."

"He's an excellent surgeon. You're in good hands." He wished me a speedy recovery and left.

The rest room was extremely clean. Every hospital or medical facility, large or small, has a characteristic odor to it, particularly in the restrooms. To some it is repulsive to the point of causing nausea and even vomiting. I have seen people faint from this smell. Exposure to hospitals for the past thirty-five years has dulled my olfactory perception, and now a hospital smells like home to me. More than half my life has been spent in hospitals. This small suburban hospital was kept very clean. In my mind I commended the housekeeping department for a job well done.

I walked back to the cubical, lay down on the gurney and started thinking about my surgery. I was going to be called any moment now. My heart began to beat faster and faster, speeding up as if it were ready to leap out of my chest. My nerves tightened like strings of a musical instrument wound so tautly around the pegs, they felt ready to break any moment. My breath halted one moment and then came rapid and shallow the next.

What if I don't come back, what will happen to my body? I think my family will cremate me. I can see my body in a casket. My family, friends and colleagues gathered in the funeral home. I am not certain if it is an open viewing or a closed one. I hope it is open so that I can see who came, but I am dead, lifeless, pale as a ghost, expressionless as a stone. Am I really important to anyone? Do people really care to see me like that? Perhaps, Manju, my son and my family will be in a state of shock and rather have me hidden behind the wooden plank of the casket.

One of my friends might ask, "What happened to him? He had knee surgery and died. He was a doctor."

"So? Are doctors special? Do they have a 'never die' privilege?"

"They think they do. Definitely, some of them do" my friend might reply with a smirk.

I could imagine Manju sitting in the front row of the funeral parlor. Her eyes would be swollen, tears rolling down uncontrollably. In my fantasy she wiped the tears with a Kleenex, but they wouldn't stop. I saw her get some more tissues from her hand bag. She still had those pretty finger nails, always neatly polished. *I am sorry honey to leave you like this. Hey, Manju, I am here. I love you so much.* She looked around to see who said that. *It's me, Neeraj.* She smiled softly, somehow maintaining her composure, which was very hard for her to do. She enjoyed laughter, fun and good times, not this. I was going away for good.

Can I move closer? This box is too tight. There is no room to maneuver. They were really trying to save money making it. Why wouldn't they? Who wants to spend money on a dead body?

I tried harder to move and almost fell from the stretcher. Somebody shook me and I realized that the nurse was looking at me rather oddly, "Mr. Bhushan, are you alright? Please be careful. You don't want more problems by falling from the stretcher. You're going for surgery any minute."

"I'm sorry." I said.

It will be all right, Dr. B. I tell myself repeatedly, but the sinking feeling does not go away. *While I am here, alive, I must find a way to connect to God. This is the only relationship where there is no pain and suffering. There is only Love. I will try to lead a simple, God friendly life and try not to worry about the circus going on around me. This circus was there before I came into existence, it is here to stay and will continue when I am gone. I am human, I have committed mistakes and I have fallen from His Grace. Whatever time God has given me here on earth, I must strive to do better than the previous day.*

Maybe I should pray more often. Why didn't I pray before in good times? Why do I think of prayer more during troubled or difficult moments? Maybe, I have to change my way of praying to God. I hope the Dear Lord will forgive me one more time.

Chapter 16

OPREATING ROOM

Lying on the stretcher, waiting for the OR tech, I felt so foreign to all the surroundings, equipment and personnel. I felt far away, alone among strangers. There was so much hustle and bustle, movement and noise, but no one was really concerned about me. The technicians, nurses and the anesthesiology staff were all occupied with preparing for surgery, not with the individual lying on the gurney. They set up the instruments, medicines and the IV's for a specific surgical procedure, but not for any special individual. Many patients like me have come through these doors. I desperately wanted someone to talk to me and reassure me that I would be fine. I was terrified about what was going to happen next. One moment I yearned to get it over with, the next moment I wanted to run out of the hospital.

Doubt and faith took turns churning my insides. *Maybe I should quietly walk out of here. No one will notice. Every one is busy anyway.* I was seriously considering this when the OR tech showed up and said, "Mr. Bhushan, You're next."

This is it. Now I can't go anywhere. The nurse and the tech wheeled me down the hallway out of the holding area and into the operating room.

It felt strange lying on the stretcher and being moved. At home, I could lie in a bed that was stationary, with a familiar ceiling and surroundings. But here I moved on wheels, and the ceiling wasn't in a fixed position. Hospital employees, people in hallways, and all other objects were perpendicular to my view. I was moving at a different speed, just a few feet above ground. Within a few short moments, we arrived at the operating room. The OR technician pressed the remote device on the wall and big doors flung open so we could enter another holding area, from which I would be taken to the operating suite.

The OR nurse came over and patted my arm. "Is this patient Bhushan?"

"Yes." The pre-op nurse said, extending my file to her. "Here are all the consent forms." She turned to me, adding "All the best, Mr. Bhushan."

The OR tech and the nurse helped me transfer from the stretcher to the operating table. I knew the exchange of information about the patient was a routine process. Now I was on the operating table. This was the final destination for surgery. *No going back now.*

My mind was going at lightning speed. It felt as if the neurons in my brain were exchanging information at a pace unknown to mankind. Conflicting thoughts churned without end in my mind, marching along without a checkpoint. I was amazed at the power of my mind when it started to think of all that could go wrong, *Complications during anesthesia, during surgery, post-op complications, blood clots and infections.* Not only that, I started looking at each complication and the cascade of events that would lead to even more trouble. Death was not far from my thoughts.

I saw so many patients everyday, and consulted for surgeons regularly for post-op complications, particularly blood clots and infections. Blood clots occurred quite often after an orthopedic procedure. They could start in the calf or thigh and quickly migrate to the lungs, causing sudden shortness of breath and chest pain. It was a serious complication. Sometimes it could be missed and if not diagnosed and treated promptly, it could be fatal. My thoughts were now completely wrapped up in this dreadful complication. I was thinking of I.V. blood thinner, Heparin, and how likely it would be that I'd have to stay a few more days in the hospital, all for a simple routine outpatient procedure. Of course, one of the common complications of I.V. Heparin was internal bleeding, which was definitely moving across my mind's radar screen . . . If I started bleeding internally; my red blood count would go down. I'd go into shock. They'd have to give me a blood transfusion. If they didn't find my blood type, I'd go into cardiac arrest. They'd start CPR.

They are pumping on my chest. My heart has an erratic disorganized rhythm. The anesthesiologist says, "Everyone move!" He uses electric paddles to bring my rhythm back, but no avail. I am dying. Please bring blood quickly, the right kind of blood. God help me please. I am going to die soon.

I hoped they'd find the right group and a clean unit of blood. I'd seen patients with Hepatitis C and HIV infection from blood transfusions. I hoped it wouldn't happen to me.

My heart rate accelerated. I said to myself: *Dummy, you haven't had the surgery yet. Are you crazy? What are you doing to yourself? Slow down, Dr. B, slow down. You can't have all possible complications; May be one or two, but not all. These are your colleagues. These are reputable doctors and nurses. They know how to manage complications. Have faith and take a deep breath.*

I composed myself and began to pray, to submerge myself in conversation with Almighty God and contemplate the countless ways I have been blessed.

Chapter 17

MY CALLING

There is a clear-cut demarcation between the mundane and spiritual world. The more I was entrenched in the mundane world; the further the spiritual world retreated from my mind. Once I gained access to the spiritual side of life, this world appeared fickle and transitory. The trouble was that my life was passing in this 'real' world, which in reality was 'unreal', changing every moment. Even though I knew this, my mind felt unsettled, unable to figure out the comfortable corner where it could hide in peace.

The OR suite was chillier than the pre-op holding area. It was a much bigger room, about fifteen by twenty feet, with a lot of personnel, two nurses, two technicians, a nurse anesthetist, an anesthesiologist and even more machinery, gadgets and equipment. Everyone seemed to be occupied, moving around the room, busy with their tasks. Dressed in green O.R. scrubs with caps and masks, I hoped they knew what they were doing. For a moment, it felt I was on another planet, and these strange looking creatures were going to do something to me. They operated on many patients every day. It was like a robotic lab. There was very little conversation. Everything was mechanized; and much of the procedure was no more than a routine for them. I wished they would say 'Hi, How are you? Don't worry, everything will be alright.' But this was precious, expensive OR time and they had a lot to do. *Just stay quiet and don't disturb them. Are they really concerned about my illness? Can I trust them? I'm totally helpless and at their mercy. Oh! I have no under garments; only a thin hospital gown; A partially clad well-known doctor. They will all see me fully naked in a few minutes, and laugh and crack jokes and pass all sorts of comments. Oh my God, my privacy is being invaded.* Emotions engulfed me. I looked at the operating room ceiling and saw two big round bright lights. These were the lights which would be used by the surgeon for a clear sharp view of the operating field.

I wanted to scream for help. *Why aren't words coming out of my mouth? Is there any one listening? No one is saying any thing. Where has everyone gone? I am alone. Please help me Lord. Please help me. I beg you, help me please.*

I looked at these bright lights in anxiety and panic. The lights became brighter and brighter, when I heard a voice.

"Son! Why are you so worried? I am here with you."

For a moment I wondered if I were hallucinating. The lights became even brighter; almost blinding, and the voice came again; *"I am here by your side, Son."*

I looked around to see who was talking to me. The OR personnel were busy. Confusion and panic choked me, and sweat beaded my forehead. *What's going on?*

"Don't be afraid, my son. I am here with you."

As I listened to this voice of comfort and reassurance for the third time, I could not resist and whispered, "Dear Lord is that you I hear? You have come to the operating room to stay by my side. Oh! Almighty . . ." words would not come out of my mouth. I wanted to say something, but could not utter a word. My chest heaved convulsively with sobs while my heartbeat pounded in my chest. I felt faint and tears filled my eyes. Somehow, I gathered myself. "Dear Lord, You are here with me?"

"Yes, my son. I am here with you."

"Dear Lord, I have not been a faithful servant. I have let you down so many times. You have come to be with me during my troubled times. If you are here with me; I don't need anyone else, I am protected from all sides, and I can endure anything. Oh! Almighty, how can I thank you? I love you Dear Lord. My heart is filled with gratitude. Oh! My savior, I will glorify your name; from East to West, North to South; everywhere on this planet, with your Grace. Dear Lord, I surrender you *all.* Thank you, Thank You for being here for me."

Dr Kaplan, my orthopedic surgeon came in and greeted me and told me that he would start in a couple of minutes. He started explaining the procedure. "We'll be making three holes in your knee." Suddenly, I felt intense pain in my left knee. Ouch! Three holes in my knee stuck in my brain, and the pain worsened, even before he finished explaining the procedure. How our minds can imagine anything; feel anything; magnify it a thousand fold, and drive everyone crazy!

Dr. Kaplan finished with his description of the procedure and said, "The anesthesiologist will give you anesthesia in a moment."

"Ok, Thanks, Tom" I replied.

A few seconds rolled by before the anesthesiologist walked into the operating room and let me know that he would start soon. He moved over to the head of the operating table to give instructions to the nurse anesthetist.

My mind was still occupied with the conversation I'd had with Almighty God. Did I hear the Lord whispering into my ear or I was imagining it? *It can't be. I heard the voice three times and I did reply to that voice. Even though it was comforting, I can't discuss it with anyone here. If I tell Dr. Kaplan or the anesthesiologist about my conversation with God, the operating room walls will reverberate with an uncontrollable laughter, echoing my stupidity even further. I'll be ridiculed all over the hospital. They'll all think I'm in dire need of a psychiatrist—not surgery on my knee. I better stay quiet.*

The nurse anesthetist standing on the right side of the operating table said, "Hi, Dr. B. My name is

Connie and I am your nurse anesthetist today." She had a mask on her face and a cap on her head. From her eyes, I could tell she was from the Orient. "We'll start the anesthesia shortly."

"Dr. B, I am going to put this mask on your face. It will cover your nose and I want you to take a deep breath."

I nodded and took a deep breath.

"Not deep enough."

So I took another deep breath.

"Not deep enough."

"Dear Lord, whatever power, strength and capacity you have given my lungs, in Your name, here is the biggest breath for You . . . . I surrender you all."

The bright lights softened and dimmed as a curtain of darkness drew over my thoughts, leaving me numb, helpless and suspended in faith.

Chapter 18

SURRENDER TO GOD

I allow the Lord to take over from here onward. Letting it free, letting it all go to that level where there is no fear, only sheer joy of His divine Grace, the invisible energy. I just keep absorbing it like a sponge. Mentally accepting the flow of this energy, and whatever that flow brings with it. The flow becomes an integral part of my existence.

I am ready to love God, to put everything on the line, even my life. It feels good to Love God, to give all of myself over to Him. I can't help it. He gave me everything. Why can't I give Him everything I have? I want to love Him more than He loves me. I came from a formless energy. I will return to that energy. The best thing which has happened to me is this understanding. I, who was nothing, who is nothing, who will be nothing, came from something that is everything. I am so happy just to know that.

I knew that surrender didn't mean giving up. It meant yielding to the higher Power, letting my power go from myself to the Supreme authority.

The smallest particle couldn't change its position without God's Grace and Power. Every day I saw sickness, suffering and pain pass through my office. Blessed were those who smiled despite the tumultuous times they were going through. They were steadfast in their faith, and I had seen them heal and walk from the clutches of death. Science had no explanation for all that I had seen. In those moments I just looked up and said *Thanks again for yet another reminder.*

I wanted to surrender to God one hundred percent, and completely give myself over to God's Will.

Dear Lord, You are the river of love. I am a log of wood floating away in that river. I am completely surrounded by the water of Your love. The river flows through the mountains, rocks and valleys, meandering through the undulations of the landscape. I am floating with You. I go where You take me. You are steering this log and You are the navigator. How lucky I am to have You, dear Lord, at the controls. I am not worried; I am not concerned. I am completely under Your control. Your destination is my destination. I have no fear, no anxiety, as You take me along. What else does anyone need? I am fast asleep, completely submerged in the river of Your love. Oh! What a wonderful feeling it is. Dear Lord, please keep me with You all the time. I will not complain. I don't need anyone if I have you.

I know sometimes worldly attachments pull me away from You. Then I think of You again, and my time in that river, when I was so clean, flowing with the water of Your love, feeling secure. You gently hold my hand and take me with You, to make me feel clean and fresh again. Time and again You come to my rescue. Dear Lord, the separation from You is very painful and You know that. I need Your help every step of the way. Let us keep this eternal connection. Dear Lord, this servant of yours will always be at your feet, ready to follow the direction You give him.

I surrendered to God's Will on the operating table, and felt the Lord by my side. His perfect hands touched my knee through the surgeon's hands.

Chapter 19

RECOVERY ROOM

About two and a half hours later I heard some noise. *Where am I? Who are these people around me? They are talking, but I don't understand what they are saying. What are they saying and to whom?* The voices appeared to be coming from far away. Apparently, the OR tech and the nursing staff were talking about transferring me to the post-anesthesia care unit. I was in a semiconscious state of mind. I opened my eyes with some effort, but my vision was blurred, and I felt as if I were looking through mist or smoke.

I was in a twilight zone, not certain where I was. *Was I moving or lying still in one place? What was going on? I don't see anyone I know.* With my hands, I tried to feel what I was lying on. It felt like a bed. No. It felt like a stretcher. I wasn't dreaming. I was on wheels, surely, on a stretcher again, floating away. A set of doors suddenly appeared beyond my feet. I thought that my feet were going to strike the door and I was going to get hurt. I said, "Please be careful." My visual acuity was impaired and depth and distance perception was abnormal. The OR tech informed me that I was being transferred to the PACU—Post-anesthesia Care Unit. The double doors opened and I saw the staff of PACU as the OR tech handed over the operating room records to the nurse. These records contained details of the surgery, including vital signs, blood and fluid loss as well as any complications. This was important information for the PACU accepting nurse. I hoped my surgery went well and there were no complications. *How can I find out? It must be noted in the OR records in my folder. Shall I ask the OR tech? Will he give me the information? I feel so weak. Maybe a short nap would help. Can I sleep or do I have to be awake for the staff?*

The nurse came over to me. "Hi Dr. B, I am Kay; your nurse here at the post-anesthesia care unit; how are you feeling?"

"I'm fine." My thoughts were not at all clear. I wasn't certain about my location, physically or mentally. *Did I have a conversation with God? Why would He come, just for me? He has so many to look after. I am not special. I haven't done anything extraordinary. But I heard Him three times! No one has ever called me 'son'. My father always called me by my first name and he passed away January 1, 1979. No one has ever addressed me with such love. Should I talk to anyone about what happened? Should I tell the nurse? No! I can't do that. She will laugh and say that I'm hallucinating. It will be embarrassing. Maybe it's the effect of anesthesia. Wait a minute. This occurred before I had the anesthesia. So it must be true. I'll stay quiet and tell Manju about it later.*

In the midst of thinking all this I dozed off. I woke up forty-five minutes later in a recliner chair and had no recollection of how I'd been transferred from the stretcher to this comfortable chair, with my feet elevated and the crutches by my side. *Am I somewhere else or in the same hospital?*

I looked around for clues until the nurse came in and said, "Look who I brought with me."

Manju was standing right behind her; a bit apprehensive, but happy to see me. She was hesitant to come close, but after seeing me smile, she came and hugged and kissed me and asked, "How are you? Are you okay? Are you in pain?"

I thought for a moment and took stock of different parts of my body, especially my legs. I felt no pain anywhere. Surprised and a bit confused, I replied, "I feel fine. I have no pain . . . yet."

I could see relief in her eyes, "I am happy to see you. Thank God, you are not in pain."

I thought, *Maybe it's the effect of the anesthetic, lingering in the pain center of my brain.* In the middle of the conversation, I fell asleep again.

Pressure on my bladder woke me up and I asked the nurse where the restroom was. She pointed towards it and said, "Let me bring your crutches. You'll need assistance."

She picked up the crutches that were leaning against the wall and held them out. "We'll help you."

I pushed the blanket aside; got up from the recliner and stood up on my operated leg. It felt fine.

"I don't think I need these." I walked to the bathroom without any help from anyone and certainly without crutches.

I felt no pain what so ever.

Manju and the nurse ran after me as I walked briskly to the restroom. They said, "Please slow down. Let us help you."

I walked without pain, without struggle, as if nothing had happened.

They looked bewildered as they watched me walk without any support. I came back from the restroom and sat in my recliner.

As I leaned back in the recliner it dawned on me what I had just done. I walked to the bathroom and back without any pain or help. I didn't use any support. *How is that possible? I did have the surgery today or didn't I?*

I felt my leg underneath the blanket. There was a big bandage from my thigh to my calf. Was it a dream? *I'm sleepy. Maybe a nap will clear things for me.*

As I was dozing off, my orthopedic surgeon came in to check on me. "Raj, the surgery went very well," he said. "There were no complications. I didn't have to remove the meniscus."

I felt a little relieved by that news.

"The torn piece was removed and I shaved the edge. It looked smooth again, like the original. By the way, you required a lot of anesthetic to put you under; almost two and a half times what we normally give for this procedure. I was getting really concerned about your post-op recovery after that much anesthesia. Are you having any pain in your knee?"

"No" I said, "None whatsoever, Tom. I feel fine."

He smiled, looked me in the eyes and said, "Wait 'til you go home. The pain is going to get much worse. I'll leave a prescription for Vicodin painkiller. Has the orthopedic-tech explained how to use the crutches?"

"Yes" I replied, "the crutches are right here."

"You'll need them for the first few days; maybe even a week." He asked Manju to set up a follow-up appointment with him the following week in his office. He wished me well, told me to call him if I had any questions and left.

I listened to his instructions carefully. I still had no pain and felt absolutely fine. After a few minutes while Manju was talking to the nurse, I started to wonder, *how is this possible that I have no pain? I remember having a conversation with God when I was on the operating table. I surrendered myself to Him. Did He really accept me, with all my faults and shortcomings? Did he give me refuge under His wings? I have been touched and blessed by Him.*

I was scared to talk about it, though deep down, I knew. I had connected with the Almighty that day.

Chapter 20

HOLY FATHER

Recently a well-known and respected saint from India was on a spiritual journey to the United States. I had listened to his audiotapes and watched his DVD's from previous spiritual retreats. Mentally and spiritually I had been connected to this learned saint for many years. It had been my dream to see him in person for quite a while, but the opportunity never arose.

In May of 2007, about eighteen months after my surgery, I was in between patients when the office manager told me that my mother was on the phone. She had been watching television when she happened to see a clip for this saint's discourse in the United States. It was a ten second advertisement, and all she could decipher from it was that the discourse would take place somewhere in Maryland. The rest of the day I saw patients with a smile plastered on my face, bubbling with joy. I could not sit still. All I could think about was going home to try to get more information about his arrival in the U.S. The ad had aired on Channel TV Asia.

At eight-thirty that night, I waited for the evening news. The very first commercial break had another clip on Saint '*Bapu*'—meaning 'Respected Holy Father.' He was coming to Maryland on July 14th, 2007 for a nine-day discourse on the Holy book. I quickly jotted down the telephone number to get further information, and sat there in a state of awe. *His holiness is coming so close to where we live. I have been dreaming about this for years. He is coming, oh, My God. Oh, My God.* I sat there and stared at the television until my vision blurred with gratitude. "I can't believe this" I kept repeating, "Thank you, Dear God."

I dialed the number for more information on the event. The gentleman who answered the phone confirmed, "Yes, *Bapu* is coming to Maryland."

"Can you please tell me who will sponsor this event? I want to help as a volunteer in any possible way."

"I can't give you that information because we are expecting two to three thousand people every day for the nine days. The sponsor has been inundated with phone calls from all over Canada, the UK, Europe and the US. This will be *Bapu's* only visit away from India this year."

Humbly I begged him to reconsider. "I have been waiting to see *Bapu* for a very long time. I would appreciate any information you could give me."

"I'll give you the name of the sponsor, but I can't give you his phone number," he said.

"That will be helpful. Thank you so much for your help."

"Hope to see you at the event."

"My wife and I will be there."

We had planned a vacation to go to the beach for the week of July 4th in North Carolina. We cancelled our reservation and decided to go for this once in a lifetime spiritual retreat.

I found the telephone number of the sponsor through the Internet. Initially I was hesitant to call, but the force inside me was strong. Nothing was going to stop me. I needed to meet and serve His Holiness in person.

When the sponsor Mr. Munger answered the phone, I introduced myself and explained to him my love and devotion for *Bapu*. I told him I'd been listening to *Bapu's* audio's and DVD's for many years, and had been waiting for this day. "Please tell me what I can do to help in any capacity." To my surprise, he was as friendly as if I had known him for years.

"Dr. B, we have our volunteers meeting at the event site day after tomorrow. Please come over. We would love to meet you."

The volunteers had met several times before and the responsibilities had already been assigned. There were fourteen attendees and I did not know anyone of them. The invitation to attend the meeting was through a phone contact. Initially it was odd sitting amongst strangers who had all known each other for years, but I had the pure burning selfless desire to serve. It was not just a desire but also a need to serve in any capacity I could. My intent was to be there as a volunteer, prepared to do whatever was asked of me.

The event coordinator saw the love and devotion in me and invited me to the next meeting ten days later. We met again, and this time everyone was friendlier. They shared the details of the event and listened to my suggestions. The meeting adjourned after two hours. After the meeting, I was approached by the coordinator and another senior member of the group.

"Dr. B, we've been thinking and talking amongst ourselves about who should be the master of ceremonies for this huge event. We're expecting a lot of people. We want you to be the master of ceremonies."

My legs went numb, my heart filled with joy and my eyes were wet with gratitude. "Really? You feel I am capable of this?" I sat in the chair for a moment, stunned, then rose and thanked the volunteer group for trusting me with this big responsibility. "I will do my best and make this event a huge success."

"Yes, Dr. B. We feel very comfortable with our choice. Please accept it as your calling. We'll discuss the agenda for the commencement for this function tomorrow. Call us and we'll review this further."

"Thanks, Dr. B, for accepting this responsibility."

"Thank you for trusting me for this huge event."

In my mind, I was certain I could handle the task. I was excited to be on the same podium and so close to *Bapu*—'His holiness.'

To this day, I get goose bumps thinking about how it happened. Here I was an unknown volunteer who was asked to become a key player in the co-ordination of an event of tremendous magnitude. It had taken eleven years for the sponsor of this event to be blessed by this saint's agreement to come to United States.

People came from all over the United States, Canada, United Kingdom and Europe to attend this enormous event. My contribution was miniscule, but my faith took a leap of unimaginable proportion.

Chapter 21

POST-OP

The nurse came in and checked my vital signs. "Everything looks good. How is the pain, Dr. B; do you need anything?"

I smiled and said "No! No pain. I'm feeling better. I'm ready to be discharged from the hospital."

"I'll call Dr. Kaplan and give him the report. I have to get the discharge orders from him." She left to look at my chart and to fill out the discharge papers.

My son Alex had gone to the local pharmacy to pick up the prescription for Vicodin. While we were waiting for the discharge papers, Manju asked me again if I had any pain in my knee.

"None," I said.

She shook her head in disbelief. I had to tell her what happened at the operating table.

Manju stood near my recliner surveying the recovery area, collecting my belongings and browsing through the discharge papers. I lay there comfortably watching her movements, and the tiny smile on her face that told me she was happy to be packing up to go home. My thoughts drifted to what I experienced in the last few hours. My reverie with God was periodically interrupted by her questions pertaining to the discharge and the follow-up appointment.

Dear Lord, How can I thank you for what you have done for me today? I cry to show my love for you. I smile to show my love for you. I want to follow your guidance and never leave it ever again. I don't know what I can do to show my gratitude. You are my rescuer. I will look for your direction to continue walking the path you have chosen for me. But Oh! Almighty, I am so afraid to talk about this to anyone. People will laugh at me. They all know I am a doctor, practicing medicine for twenty-five years. How can I convince them of your magical Power and Grace? Please help me. I know you have touched me today. The sensation of your love passes through every pore of my body like electricity. I feel dizzy, completely enveloped in your love.

Manju started to put my belongings in a bag. "Do you need help to change into your street clothes?"

I looked at her, smiled and said, "I'm feeling fine. I'll be able to manage myself." I rose from the recliner, took off the hospital gown, put on my clothes and felt ready to walk out of the hospital.

The nurse came in and said, "You can't go out like this. We have to get you in a wheelchair. Here are your crutches."

Wheelchair and crutches! Do I really need them? I have no discomfort. Who needs wheelchair and crutches? But I can't tell the nurse. It is best to stay quiet for now, so I'll follow the code and keep everyone happy.

Wait a minute. The force inside me to talk about God is too strong to hold back. I have to say something otherwise I will explode.

Hold your horses, Dr. B. Talk about it later.

But I can't. I have to speak about God's Power.

Everyone is busy right now. Maybe later!

So I sat down quietly on the wheelchair. Manju took all the instructions from the nurse and I was wheeled out of the hospital. Our car was already parked at the entrance where the valet had brought it earlier. I got up from the wheelchair and stood by the car, looked back at the hospital, then looked up in the sky in total disbelief. Was it a day of surgery or the beginning of a spiritual journey?

I thanked the nurse for her excellent, kind and compassionate care during my brief stay at the same-day surgery center.

While I sat on the passenger side of the car, we moved slowly as we left the pavilion medical building. I had been on wheels earlier in the day, mostly on the stretchers in the pre-op, post op recovery area, and in the hallways of the hospital. This time I rode on a different set of wheels; in the car, in an upright position. The surgery went well. No post op complications and no pain. I couldn't ask for anything more. As we drove out from the hospital campus; the red Emergency Room sign on the right slowly faded away from my sight.

I sat in the car, watching the scenery outside, the falling leaves, defoliated trees, and cars passing by on the highway. The world around me moved at its usual pace. I didn't want to look towards Manju or start a conversation with her. I wanted to hide my emotions from her as we drove back home. I was happy and sad at the same time, as if I were riding an emotional roller coaster. I felt like opening the window and shouting to the world, '*I found IT. I found God. He came to see me today.*' My inner joy had no limits and boundaries. At times, my eyes were wet.

Why me Lord? Why me? This phrase hammered at me incessantly. *What did I do to deserve this miracle? Is it premature to say a miracle really did occur in the operating room?* Baffled, a seesaw of emotions shook my faith and belief to the core and left me completely drained. I sat in the car, locked in the maze of emotions, not knowing where this experience was going to lead me. *Why did all this happen to me? What is my purpose in life? What am I supposed to do now?*

Chapter 22

RECOVERY AT HOME

As we drove home, I watched the passing scenery and thought of God again and again as I admired the beautiful sunny day, blue skies and His wonderful creation around me.

I turned and looked at the back seat of the car. The crutches weren't there—I'd intentionally left them at the hospital because I didn't need them. The best support stood by me and lifted me up. *How could you Lord? I have sinned in my lifetime; you have forgiven me. You have blessed me. You have taken my pain away. You have healed my knee with your touch. I am sorry; so sorry for not being your best student.* Tears started rolling down my cheeks. They wouldn't stop. I felt as if I had let down my best friend—Almighty God.

Manju was watching me. "Are you in pain?"

"No my dear, I'm fine."

"Then why are you crying?"

"I'm not crying. It's hard to explain. These are tears of joy for the Lord's Grace on me, tears because the Lord took away the burden of my pain. I just feel blessed. I feel it inside me. Maybe one day you'll realize what I mean at this moment." With a gentle smile I said, "Please don't worry, I am fine."

She was surprised to see my reaction and started shaking her head. "You're crazy," she muttered jokingly.

How could I tell her what was going on in my brain? How could I tell her what I had witnessed, and how deeply I felt the birth of my passion for our Dear Lord? Would she understand? My faith had taken a blind, astronomical leap. It was magical. Electricity ran through my body, my muscles quivered, my hair stood on end. I felt like jumping in ecstasy. Joy and inner peace flooded my body and soul. Oh my God, it felt phenomenal. As I write this I feel the miracle happening again all over again. The same elation lifts me to the heights and makes me fly through the clouds. I feel so blessed. *Thank you. Thank you.*

We exited the highway and turned into our subdivision. It was a beautiful early fall afternoon. The sun was setting in the western sky and the denuded trees made the contour of the landscape much clearer. The houses which had been hidden behind the lush green of the past few months were now visible in the neighborhood. The road leading to our house was full of fallen leaves, some fresh, some decaying, reminding me of the cycle of birth and death.

Our house sat at the end of the cul-de-sac, and I could see Mom sitting by her bedroom window, eyes focused on the street, eagerly awaiting our arrival. Manju opened the garage door, parked the car, looked at me and said, "You think you'll be able to get out of the car? Or do you want me to come around and help you?"

"I can manage." I slid easily out of the car, walked into the kitchen and greeted Mom.

Her cheeks sagged and her mouth trembled as she studied me. "How are you feeling? Come in and sit down."

"Mom, I'm fine."

"How could you be fine? You just had surgery today. Don't just stand there; sit down. Let me get you something to drink."

My mouth was dry and I was thirsty from a long day at the hospital. The anesthesia and all the other medicines had parched my lips and tongue. When she offered me a glass of water, I drank it in one long gulp. She gave me a kiss and said "God Bless you! You must be tired. Go in your bedroom and lie down, you need rest."

"I'll see you later, Mom."

I walked away from the kitchen and entered our bedroom through the study. The emerald green carpet, sea green walls and the high-coffered ceiling gave the room a cool, comforting feel. Two large windows overlooked the wooded backyard. The king-size bed looked inviting after a long day at the hospital. The presence of God, peace and solace filled the room and made it feel special. I changed into pajamas and got into bed.

Mom and Manju came into the bedroom, looking concerned, staring at me as if they wondered what I was hiding. "How are you feeling?" Mom asked.

"I feel fine. I have no pain, Mom. Please don't worry."

"You're hiding something from us. How could you have no pain? You just had surgery today."

"It's true. I have no pain. I don't know what else I can tell you."

"Did the surgeon say anything? Were there any problems or complications during surgery?"

"He said that the surgery went well and I would be back on my feet within a week." It felt weird saying this, since I was already on my feet. I had walked into the house and to my bedroom without any assistance, as if no surgery had taken place today.

"That is strange. You have no pain?" Mom wondered. "When do you see the surgeon again?"

"Next week."

As I tried to reassure them that everything went well and I felt fine, they shook their heads in disbelief.

I decided to keep my conversation with God to myself for a little while longer. I wanted to rest and mull over what had happened earlier in the day. What occurred in the OR still puzzled me, and I wasn't sure what to make of it. Was it a dream, or had my true calling arrived? Had I become a victim of faith and doubt both at the same time? I was excited. I felt healed, physically as well as spiritually, and my inner joy couldn't be contained. Yet I felt uncomfortable talking about it with my family. What had happened felt precious, fragile, and I wanted to keep it locked deep inside me. Maybe my lack of faith in the past made me doubt the miracle I had witnessed. I'd just been through a very unusual experience, and I wanted to imbibe it fully. The fear that something could go wrong still lurked in my subconscious and stopped me from telling anyone what I had experienced. It felt premature to talk about this miracle, and in the deepest part of me I still questioned God's role in what had happened.

My son Alex had picked up the prescription from the pharmacy for the painkiller Vicodin, and the vial of pills sat on the nightstand next to my bed.

When Mom and Manju came in to check on me, I said "Here is the painkiller, but I'm not in any pain." She smiled, but I saw concern on her face as she studied me. I knew she expected me to grimace with pain at any moment, and then she could advise me to take the painkiller. Clearly she was uncomfortable not doing anything for me, and she obviously thought that I was hiding my pain from her so she wouldn't worry.

"Well, we are happy to see you are feeling as well as you say you are."

After an hour of watching me carefully, seeing me relaxed and not in any distress, she finally felt at ease. Manju brought me a cup of warm milk. I drank the milk more to satisfy them than to quench my thirst.

My brother and in-laws came over in the evening to see me in person. When Manju's parents came in, I stood up and greeted them. They stopped dead in their tracks when they saw me stand without assistance, and their eyes widened as they surveyed my posture from top to bottom. "You're standing? Did you really have surgery today? You look too good for someone who was operated on six hours ago." When they saw me walk without difficulty, they were shocked. Of course they wanted to know how my surgery went, and if there were any problems. My brother said "Hey Raj, please lie down, you just had the surgery today. Don't stress yourself."

I replied, "According to the surgeon, everything went well. I feel fine." To put them at ease, I lay down with my left leg elevated.

He joked, "You do look fine. Are you sure you had surgery today?"

"No! I thought I'd play sick today and let everybody pamper me."

"How many days do you plan to get pampered?"

"I go back to work on Monday. Maybe, half a day depending on how I feel."

"When is your follow-up visit?"

"Dr. Kaplan will remove the stitches next Tuesday."

They stayed for an hour with us and wished me a speedy recovery. I got up to say goodbye to them, and then went back to bed. I was still perplexed by my experience in the hospital. It was eerie, and a wide swing of emotions tossed me. I felt a deep empathy for others in pain, and wondered why they suffered while I received this preferential treatment. Surgery had been a painless journey for me so far, but I was afraid of what was coming next. Was this the calm before the storm? Was something really bad hiding behind all this? Excitement about this miracle made me want to tell the world, but the fear of what might happen sealed my lips. I decided to stay quiet.

Manju went to the kitchen to prepare dinner. It was time for me to connect with Almighty God, one on one, and witness the magic with no one around. I felt so good that I started to doubt I had surgery at all. I wondered what everyone would say if I asked that question. Surely they would say that I was being foolish. How could I doubt the reality of the last twenty-four hours? I was in the hospital. I went through registration, pre-op, time in the operating room and then in the recovery room. Manju was certainly tired after a long day in the surgical waiting area at the hospital, and she witnessed everything. *I did have the surgery today. Don't be stupid, just lie down and rest.*

As I lay in bed in solitude, my mind wandered over all my faults and shortcomings. How was this possible, after all that I'd done wrong in my life? *Why was I spared from pain and suffering? Why did this happen?*

Chapter 23

CONNECTING WITH GOD

One day, years before my surgery, as I sat on the Cardiac floor in the hospital, completing my daily patient chart review, the senior partner from a large cardiology practice came to the nursing station. After exchanging pleasantries, he pulled up a chair and sat next to me to review a patient's chart. He had a beautiful gold watch on his wrist, a Rolex. My mind zeroed in on his watch. I wished I had a watch like that. I reviewed the chart of my patient, but my mind kept drifting towards that watch. I was more consumed by the timekeeper on his wrist than I was concerned about my patient. I wanted to know how much that watch was worth. I knew those watches were expensive, perhaps worth thousands of dollars. I stayed in that chair and engaged him in conversation, just to study that ornament on his wrist a little longer. He probably wondered why I was friendlier that day than my usual quiet demeanor. I had an ordinary timepiece on my wrist. Although I wanted to compliment him on his watch, I was afraid of what he would think of me when he saw mine. Would he still respect me as a colleague or would my watch isolate me from his friendship? I knew him as a respected cardiologist, probably a very rich one too. His watch said it all: *This is success.* Maybe I'd be successful too, if I had that beautiful watch.

As I sat at the nursing station totally consumed by envy, I felt as if everyone around me, particularly my professional colleagues, would view me differently if I had a Rolex on my wrist. Driving back home that watch stuck in my mind like a thorn.

At dinner I made a comment to Manju about the watch.

She said, "Maybe you should get one for yourself. I know it's expensive, but you work hard." In my mind I started justifying the purchase of the watch, assuring myself that I deserved it.

Manju bought me a Rolex on my fiftieth birthday.

At first I was very excited about it. I knew I had climbed the ladder of success. Everyone would notice my watch and my status would be higher than all those out there who didn't have one. I was part of an elite club, and now I could show it off at parties and get-togethers. I knew I'd feel different with that watch on my wrist.

Wait a minute, Dr. B, how is it any different? It tells me the time like any other watch. Time is the same for me and everyone else out there; nothing special. Is my life any different with this watch? How have I forgotten the invisible timekeeper, who knows my timetable, who knew my time of arrival and knows my time of departure? Let Him guide me throughout my day, and throughout my life. Let me try His timetable for a while.

After a while I put the watch back in the box because I felt uncomfortable wearing it. It didn't change me as a person. Now I smile at my stupidity, and hate the superciliousness and disdain that caught me in the deadly sins of pride and envy.

Chapter 24

CUROSITY

I heard the sounds of pots and pans in the kitchen. Manju was busy cooking. This was the precise time for me to see what was done in the operating room today. Quietly, I got up and walked to the bathroom. The master bathroom was farthest from the kitchen, and I knew no one could hear me in there.

I walked back and forth a few times, bent my knee, and felt no pain. The knee felt fine. Still, I had to check it. I sat down on the step to the bath tub and took my pajamas off. A big bandage extended from my mid thigh to mid calf. Slowly I opened the bandage until half way through, when I thought to myself, *why am I doing this? What if something happens and I mess it up? But I still can't believe I had surgery today. I have no pain and my knee actually feels better than it did before the surgery. I need to know for sure if I was operated on today.* I paused for a moment, rewrapped the bandage and sat there, unable to decide what to do.

Curiosity finally overpowered me. I had to know. *You're a doctor; what can go wrong? Don't be afraid, see it for yourself or you won't be able to sleep tonight.* Slowly, I started to remove the bandage again. Underneath this bandage was the adhesive bandage covering my left knee. Around the edges of this bandage, I saw yellow discoloration from the iodine antiseptic, where my knee had been thoroughly cleaned before the operation. As I removed the adhesive tape, I felt excitement, fear and a degree of uncertainty. Was I doing the right thing? *Will Dr. Kaplan be upset with me if he finds out? He's supposed to un-wrap the bandage and check the wound, not me.* Cautiously, I unpeeled the adhesive tape, my vision magnified so that every little line and indentation was clearly visible. They had shaved my knee and the adjoining area. It looked different, all stained yellow compared with the light brown skin on the other knee.

The stitches of the first wound became visible as I continued peeling off the bandage, and then the second wound and then the third wound came into view. I pulled the adhesive bandage completely off. To my utmost surprise, I saw three sutured wounds on my knee. *How is this possible?* I felt lightheaded, dizzy, in a state of shock. I did have the surgery. There was hardly any swelling around the stitched area. It looked fine, except for the three stitched areas and the yellow discoloration from iodine.

What happened? Why is there no pain? It is a miracle. I sat on the side of the bathtub, looking at my operated knee.

As a doctor, I know about the anatomy of the knee, muscles and nerves. Typically, after a surgery there is swelling, pain and stiffness around the wound because the tissues have been pulled and traumatized. It should feel heavy, as if lead has been infused into the joint. It should feel much larger, bigger than the other side. Usually it stiffens up, and the flexibility of the joint is far less. And of course, there is pain associated with the surgery. Tissues have been cut and holes have been drilled into the knee joint, so this means it has to be painful.

I had three holes drilled into my knee, but I had no pain. I had surgery and I felt fine. Just a few hours before, the surgeon shaved off the torn medial meniscus, cleaned the area and sutured it together, but I had no pain. *Take a deep breath and calm down. You are making a big deal out of all this. Wait for a bit longer. The pain will come back with a vengeance.* But now I doubted that it would. The conversation with God seemed very real, and the consequences of that conversation were present in front of me, leaving me speechless.

I couldn't explain this medically, so there had to be a spiritual touch to all this. *Oh my God, Oh my Lord,* I thought, bowing my head. I covered my face with both hands as I trembled, tears rolling down my face uncontrollably.

Dear Lord, thank you. Please forgive me for not listening to your word. I surrender to you from this day on, and

I will do everything in Your name. While I prayed my tears continued to flow. I sat there for I don't remember how long. I was given a new direction a few hours ago. The path was carved for my life, my future. I sat there on the bathtub step in a sublime state of God's Grace.

Gathering my emotions, I put the tape and the bandage back on my knee, then washed my face and stood there for a few minutes, soaking in the glory of Almighty God. I put my pajamas back on and came back to the bedroom to lie down. I had not taken any pain medication. The bottle of Vicodin sat next to my bed. I kept looking at it and smiled again and again, enjoying the drama that unfolded right in front of my eyes.

Manju walked in. "The dinner is ready. How do you feel, my dear?"

"I feel great. Please take this bottle of Vicodin and leave it in the medicine cabinet in the bathroom. I don't need it. I have no pain."

She looked uncomfortable with this. "I'll bring you some Tylenol instead, so you'll have medicine by your bed in the middle of the night if you're hurting."

I got up, walked to the kitchen and sat down at the dining table. With my left leg elevated, I had dinner with my family. We spent half an hour together at the dining table talking about the day's events and returned to our respective rooms.

I was lying in bed when Manju returned to the bedroom. Seeing me comfortably lying on the bed, with my eyes partially closed and a contented smile on my face, she inquired, "What are you thinking? I know you have something on your mind. What is it?"

"How do you know?" As excited as I was to tell her about my experience on the operating table, the fear of being an object of scornful laughter kept me quiet.

"I know. I can tell. Are you alright? What's going on?"

"I'm fine. There's nothing on my mind."

"Yes! There is. It's written all over your face. You're awfully quiet. Are you in pain?"

"I have to tell you something," I said.

"What is it?" Her face lost color and stillness took over her usual cheerful demeanor. I could see her brace herself for what was coming next.

"It's nothing serious."

She relaxed a bit, but I knew she was still anxious. "You scared me. What is it?"

"God came into the operating room today. I had a conversation with God."

The silence in the bedroom was broken by the burst of her laughter.

"Really, it's true." I realized what a long battle lay ahead for me to convince her of what happened earlier in the day. "He called me 'Son.' He was by my side taking care of me."

"You must have been hallucinating. You were under anesthesia."

"No . . . it happened before that."

"What did He say?" she asked seriously.

"He said 'Son, why are you afraid? I am here by your side.' It was scary, but beautiful. I surrendered myself to His Will today. It felt good. I feel so happy, as if I've been given something precious."

At first I could tell my enthusiasm bothered her. She looked at me, raised her eyebrows and shook her head, clearly dismissing the experience as the effect of the narcotics and painkiller. I articulated the whole experience to her again.

Reluctantly, she smiled and said, "Why are you worried that I will not believe you? I am with you. I'm glad you were touched by God today. I'm happy you have no pain or discomfort." After a minute, she giggled and said, "If you were hurting, you'd keep me up all night. You make a terrible patient."

Around nine-thirty that night I went to bed. In the middle of the night, I had to relieve myself. I walked to the bathroom without any problem, came back and stood by the window overlooking the back yard. It was a few minutes past midnight and the moonlight had broken the veil of darkness, though the silence and stillness of the night prevailed. For a moment, I thought I could whisper my story of the day to the silence. Would she understand the dance and drama going on within me? Would she believe me? I wanted to hold it all inside me and not share it with anyone, at least for now. It was so precious, yet something urged me to spell it out verbatim, over and over again. What was going on? What was the right thing to do? I wasn't sure. I walked back and forth a few times testing my knee.

It was dark in the room except for the highway lights visible at a distance through the windows of our bedroom. Mentally and physically exhausted, I walked quietly over to the bed. While I lay in bed I went through the events of the last twenty-four hours in a state of disbelief. *How is this possible? This really happened to me. God has chosen me today out of Billions of people. The creator has bestowed His blessings on me. The Almighty has come to my rescue; me, the one who has faltered at every step of the way. How could you, God? How could you take my pain and suffering away?*

I lay there deep in my thoughts, wondering why I received this miracle. I had seen so much pain and suffering as a doctor. To enjoy such a pain free recovery made me uncomfortable. Why had I been given this privilege?

Chapter 25

GLORIA

As I lay in bed, deep in my thoughts, I considered my patients. Those who had steadfast faith in spite of serious illness gave me reassurance and hope. Other patients I could recall gave me no comfort at all. Rather, their stories would paint a gloomy picture of life in general. The story of Gloria, a dear neighbor, friend and a patient of mine came into my mind

Gloria was a fifty-six year old Caucasian woman who came to see me in the late nineteen eighties, and her spirit touched me in a special way. She was a lady of unconditional faith, always smiling even when faced with adversities. She suffered from cirrhosis of the liver, which is usually caused by excessive alcohol ingestion. But her condition was not secondary to excessive alcohol use; on the contrary, she never drank alcohol in her life. She had non-alcoholic cirrhosis of the liver, a disease poorly understood at that time. Her condition declined over a period of twelve months. As she weakened she came to see me for persistent fatigue. Medications were not helpful, and a liver transplant was her only hope. She would always talk to me about faith and she was ready to accept whatever came her way.

Whenever I told her, "Gloria, you have a serious progressive liver disease," her favorite response was, "Dr. B, I'll be ready whenever God calls me back home. I just hope my daughter finds a good man and gets married soon."

One day, visiting me in the office, she asked me with a smile on her face, "Is there any hope for my survival? How much time do I have?" Her face was pale, and an anxious look of expectation lit her eyes with hope.

"Gloria, this is not a hopeless situation by any means," I said. "Your liver is still functioning. Medications are not helpful, we know that, but liver transplant is an option."

"*Liver transplant*" Whatever color was left on her pale face vanished. Sadness took over her usual pleasant disposition. She was quiet for a moment, then let out a deep sigh and asked, "Is there any other option for my survival, Dr. B?"

"Your disease has progressed over the past year. You can bleed from this condition in your esophagus, get infections and even go into hepatic coma if your liver fails. A liver transplant is your only option. And time is of the essence."

"Well, I guess there is no other choice. I'm not sure what I want to do. I'll discuss it with my husband and let you know. Will you talk to my husband about this?"

"Absolutely, tell him to call me with any questions."

It was late afternoon when she left my office, and at two in the morning I received a call. "Dr. B, this is Gloria. I'm not feeling well. My stomach is distended and I had a black bowel movement."

"Are you dizzy or lightheaded?"

"Yes, I am." The response was weak and barely audible.

"Call 911 and come to the Emergency Room right away. I'll meet you there."

I dressed quickly and drove to the hospital, knowing she was in trouble. She was bleeding internally, a dreadful complication of advanced liver disease. The fifteen-minute drive to the hospital seemed to take forever. After I left my car in the ER parking lot, I ran in and asked one of the nurses on duty if the paramedics had brought in Gloria.

"She's in exam room six."

As I entered exam room six, Gloria looked at me with a pale glazed look and said, "Thanks for coming, Dr. B." Her husband stood by her bedside holding her hand, looking anxious. She had vomited small amount of tarry material in a kidney tray she was barely able to hold in her hand.

"I feel nauseous, Dr. B." She was pale as a sheet. Her skin was cold and clammy. I pulled out my stethoscope to examine her, but before I could do anything, she vomited tarry material mixed with dark blood all over the bed sheet, the floor, and my shoes. Her eyes rolled back in her head. The white conjunctive and her colorless lips made me think she was going to bleed to death right there, before I could do anything.

I held her cold hand and screamed, "Nurse." Gloria barely grasped my hand with the little force left in her nearly bloodless body. She whispered, "Dr. B, will you stay with me till the end?"

"I'm here. I'm not going to leave you. I'll stay with you all the way."

When the nurse came rushing in the room, I never took my eyes off Gloria's ashen face as I said, "IV fluids wide open. I need blood for this patient, six units, STAT. Call the Gastroenterologist, Dr Shepard right away." The Normal saline IV infused 300cc of fluid, but Gloria's blood pressure was still barely palpable. She was in hemorrhagic shock.

I watched the monitor like a hawk, studying her vital signs while telling her husband what was going. All the while, I continued to hold her wrist and palpate the thready rapid pulse, hoping it would get stronger and slow down a bit.

She opened her eyes a few minutes later and said, "Dr. B, I feel so weak."

"You are hemorrhaging internally. We need to give you blood as soon as it's available from the blood bank. I've paged Dr. Shepard to come to the ER. We'll have to take you to the GE Lab for an endoscopy to find out where you're bleeding. You'll be transferred to the ICU shortly."

Eventually Gloria was transferred to ICU and underwent emergency endoscopy. She bled from esophageal varices—dilated veins in the esophagus. She stayed in the hospital for nine days, undergoing tests and evaluation for a liver transplant. Subsequently she was released from the hospital, even though she was frail and weak.

She came to see me in the office the following week. During our conversation, she exclaimed, "The Lord has some purpose for me to be around for a little while longer. Thanks so much for all your help."

I couldn't understand the level of her belief, or her conviction that Lord had the right plan for her. She wasn't afraid of death—she was just frustrated with the side effects of all the medications.

Gloria underwent a liver transplant a few months after her initial admission to the hospital. She never fully recovered and passed away a year later, but she remained strong in her faith until the end. Her husband could never understand her faith. He had a PhD from a prestigious university and had maintained meticulous records of her illness, medications and lab tests. They were so far apart; she depended on her spiritual life, while he relied on the medical sciences, technology and innovations in transplant medicine. The dichotomy of their approach to life was astounding.

Gloria's deep faith made a bigger impact on me now than it did in the eighties. This episode jumped out of my memory bank stronger than ever after undergoing my knee surgery, cementing my faith in Almighty God.

Time and again my patients impressed me with their trust in God as they faced their illnesses. Each time I witnessed their faith, it pulled me towards a larger understanding of God's magical Powers. It seemed Divine intervention always superceded medical marvels.

Chapter 26

HOME ALONE

Manju had to go to work the Wednesday before Thanksgiving. We had a light breakfast together before she left. On her way to the garage, she paused, came back and asked, "Do you want me to stay home today? Who will help you if you start having any discomfort?" I looked at her and said, "The same entity will look after me, who came to the operating room and touched me. I am fine. Don't worry about me. See, I'm walking without any problem. I'll call you and keep you posted."

I began to walk back to my bedroom when she called after me with a chuckle and said, "Could you also tell that entity to cook for me tonight?"

"Yes, I can, but He also knows that men are a mess in the kitchen. He would prefer you ask Him for that yourself."

The outer bandage on my thigh was loose because I'd opened it and played with it like a child last night. I called Dr. Kaplan's office to ask for his permission to remove the bandage. When he returned my call, he inquired if I had any pain or discomfort. I told him that I had no pain and I was walking without any support. He advised me to go ahead and remove the outer bandage, but leave the wound covered with inner adhesive tape until he could see me in his office the following Tuesday. We wished each other a Happy Thanksgiving.

Reading has always been my favorite pastime, but a busy practice and family obligations never allowed me enough spare time to fully indulge in this hobby. Today was a golden opportunity for me to pick up a nice book, sit down quietly and read for a while. I sat with my leg elevated and read 'Writing for the Soul' By Jerry Jenkins. The whole book was written on faith. Deep inside me, I heard my faith repeatedly telling me that I should write about my experience, but it was difficult to accept all that I had seen and felt so far. It seemed that my connection to the spiritual side of life had transcended medical science and healed me.

For the last thirty-five years, I'd grown within the field of medicine. I'd become an expert in the field, and I always explained the process of healing on a medical basis. Now I had to accept the fact that I'd been healed on a spiritual basis, and then try to explain it to everyone around me. Divinity had trumped the practice of medicine.

It seemed my calling had come. A higher authority had opened a new door for my spiritual growth.

'Do I believe all this?' I asked myself.

I wasn't sure. At times I thought, *yes, it's true.* At other times I still had doubt. Who should I turn to, my family, my friends or someone else who has a strong belief? No answer came to me. Mentally exhausted, I fell asleep.

I woke at four in the afternoon, feeling refreshed and energetic, and turned on the TV. *What a luxury!* I hadn't watched television at this time of day in ages. On Channel Twenty, Oprah Winfrey was talking to the famous singer Faith Hill about the song "I surrender all . . ." They discussed faith, God and spirituality. After the interview, Oprah requested Faith Hill sing this particular song. I started singing "I have surrendered all . . ." and started crying. I couldn't stop. Tears were rolling down my cheeks.

I had surrendered completely to God's Will on the operating table. It was twenty-four hours after the surgery, and I felt no pain or discomfort. I hadn't taken one tablet of painkiller. I was walking without crutches. I cried tears of joy, tears of happiness, and the tears of eternal connection continued to flow. I was glued to the TV, reliving the experience. I had goose bumps all over and my heart raced until I became light headed, as if an electric current ran through my body. The drama of spiritual ecstasy unfolding inside me was absolutely magical. For a moment, it seemed I was not lying on my bed, but floating away.

Dear Lord, you are spoiling me with your love. I feel at peace, despite my shortcomings. At times I wonder whether I deserve all this. You know it all, my Lord. I am not worthy of this. You have uplifted my body, mind and soul. I am all yours and I bow my head to you at your feet. Please hold me and keep me close to you as this is where I feel the best; the most secure. I am not afraid of anything anymore. Thank you Lord for all that you have given me. I Surrender All.

I'd been busy with the usual chores of life, just like anybody else. Running a medical practice was not an easy task. The regulations of the insurance industry and the demands from patients keep life very hectic on the business front. Family needs are equally important, and I never have time to think of God and the blessings. This was the first time I surrendered completely. I felt so ashamed of myself. Why didn't I do it before? Why have I kept God at a distance?

Still in my thoughts, I heard the garage door open as Manju came home from work. I had no idea where the last couple of hours went. I was still in bed with my left leg elevated on a pillow as she walked into the bedroom.

"How are you feeling? How was your day? What happened to the ace bandage on your leg?"

"I removed it," I replied

"Why? Did you check with Dr. Kaplan?"

"Yeah, it was getting loose and I got his permission to remove it."

"Are you having any pain? Is your leg stiff or are you able to stand and walk?"

"I'm fine, and in no pain. No stiffness. Look, I can bend my knee." I stood up and walked across the bedroom, back and forth a couple of times.

"Don't push yourself. Please get back in bed."

"I feel great, really!"

"Thank God." She smiled, her eyed wide open, bewildered yet joyous at my painless recovery, she came close and gave me a big hug, "I am so happy for you."

The second post-op day, I decided to clean my operated knee and check the wound. I sat down and cleaned my knee with saline solution. The three-sutured wounds looked clean. There was hardly any swelling, and the range of motion of the knee joint was excellent. There was no pain.

After attending to my knee, I took a long hot shower. Soothed and refreshed, I sat down at my desk in the study to check my computer for news and e-mails. I felt great. I looked at my knee and couldn't believe the surgery was only forty eight hours ago. Was it a temporary relief or had my knee really healed? *Has an angel touched me? Will it hold itself when I get back to work on Monday? Will the pain come back?*

Chapter 27

CONTEMPLATION

M onday morning I woke up early, well rested from all the sleep I had over the weekend. I showered and dressed quickly; I had cereal and milk for breakfast. Manju and Mom were concerned about my going to work only five days after the surgery. How could I convince them I felt fine? I was afraid to even talk about it. What if I jinxed it? There was definitely reason to celebrate, but I was not fully convinced myself of what had happened. I was riding the shock wave of the miracle, with doubt still lurking in the background.

There was no reason to boast, because overall it was a humbling experience. It was not an exceptional feat of my mind, but a miracle of God's Grace. This wasn't a victory—it was a reminder of my failure to follow the covenants of Almighty God. There were moments when I was less than perfect and on many occasions I fell short of what was expected of me. My mind drifted back to one of those moments.

One morning, a few years back I was in a rush to go to the hospital. I sat at the dining table for breakfast, waiting for Manju to bring the toast to the table. In her rush to get everything on the table, the toast burned. I looked at the burnt toast on my plate and felt enraged. I felt like picking it up and throwing it across the table towards the trash bin. I tried to control my temper but to no avail. I rose from the table without eating anything, infuriated; I left the house, got into my car and drove off. Manju called after me but I did not stop or talk to her.

Of course she was hurt. She had tried to rush, to get me out the door quickly. After a few minutes in the car the anger started to cool down and I felt horrible about my behavior. I knew I'd hurt her feelings, just for a piece of toast. After that day, I promised myself that I would do my best to control my temper. What would have happened if I was delayed by a few minutes? There wasn't any emergency or life-and-death situation at the office.

On the first morning I went to work after the surgery, I promised Manju that I would take it easy. I was anxious to get back to work. I wanted to see how I would do on my feet, the first day back. It was another beautiful fall day, with blue skies, puffy white clouds and a little chill in the air. It felt good to be out of the house, doing normal things. The short drive to my office was a blur as

I thanked the dear Lord and contemplated all the ways that I had been blessed.

I pulled my car into the hospital parking garage, parked, crossed the access road to the hospital, and walked to the Medical Pavilion. The walk was slightly uphill from the garage, and my office was located on the fourth floor of the building. As I entered the building, my mind drifted back to the events five days ago when I had entered the same building to have my knee fixed. As I walked at a modest pace, I was amazed at how swiftly I could navigate the walk. Pain was merely a thought in my mind, and in no way restricted my mobility. *No pain, no discomfort! It's a medical impossibility, a real miracle unfolding in my life.*

I never thought I'd be returning to work five days after surgery, walking freely as if nothing has happened. *Can I talk about this miracle? Will my office staff believe me? Maybe I will stay quiet for now.* It seemed premature to talk about it, since only five days had elapsed since my surgery.

Typically Monday was a very hectic day in the office, but Jackie, my office manager had kept a light schedule for me. Five days of rest was great, but working in the office was a different ball game. I knew I'd be continuously walking and up on my feet. Would my knee hold up to the pressure of four to five hours of standing? Would the pain start? *Has the wound really healed?*

Come on Dr. B, I scolded myself. *You witnessed the whole drama. Do you have doubts? Is your faith again in question? You remember, "I surrender all." You can't go back. You're on a different path, going in a different direction. Be*

strong. Almighty God has blessed you. You have been touched.
You are HEALED.

But why was I healed now, and not at other times earlier in my life?

My most vivid recollection of pain was the discomfort I endured with a kidney stone in 1988. I was involved in building a house. I had bought a new car. Material possessions and ego had taken a strong hold on me. God and faith were the farthest things from my mind, and I was trying to conquer the world. Forget about surrendering to anyone. I wanted everyone to surrender to my will.

Early one morning, years ago, pain in my left flank woke me up. Before long, the pain became unbearable, accompanied with nausea. Manju was scared and insisted we go to the emergency room. I was in agony. With Manju's help, I managed to put clothes on and got in the car. Lying on the back seat of the car, I couldn't get comfortable in any position. She drove me to the ER as fast as she could. The triage nurse took one look at me and put me on a stretcher right away. I was pale, diaphoretic and in distress. I was given IV fluids and narcotic painkillers that gave me relief, and I finally fell asleep.

Dr. Burger, a urologist and a colleague came over to see me. "Hey Raj, What are you doing here in the ER? I am used to seeing you taking care of patients, not being one yourself."

"Mike, it hurt like hell this morning. I feel better now. Have you seen my x-rays yet?"

"Yes. It seems you have a kidney stone. We are going to do an IVP—Intravenous Pyelogram, a dye test in the next hour. I'll come back after reviewing your IVP. If the pain returns, ask for more painkillers. I'll see you later."

The IVP revealed a five-millimeter stone (calculus) in the ureter tube, which connects the kidney to the bladder. Dr. Burger came back and said, "We'll keep you in the hospital overnight. If you have any more pain and/or the stone doesn't move, we'll have to do a cystoscopy to manipulate the stone and extract it in the next day or two." As I listened to Dr. Burger, my pain completely subsided. The procedure he explained meant putting the scope up my penis into the urinary bladder and the ureter. Suddenly I was more scared of the procedure than the pain I came in with. He advised me to pass urine through the strainer and see if the stone would pass the natural way. "I hope you have a restful night and you pass the calculus. I'll see you tomorrow."

I slept through the night. My urine flow was normal and my pain was less than before but had not subsided. My urinary obstruction was partially relieved. Either the stone had moved or the painkillers had relaxed my obstructed ureter. I hoped to be released from the hospital with instructions to drink a lot of water and take painkillers as needed.

The next morning Dr. Burger asked me, "Do you drink beer, Raj?"

"No! I don't drink alcohol. Why?"

"It's a strong diuretic and it may help you push this stone out." I came home and decided to follow up on Dr. Burger's recommendation. I had never been an alcohol drinker. I had a bad reaction to it the one time I tried a drink in my medical school days.

I picked up a six-pack of Miller-lite from the convenience store on the way home. Manju was shocked to see me try to drink beer and she said, "Don't do this. The stone will pass soon." The pain I had endured the day before was horrible, and I wanted to get rid of that stone. Sitting on the sofa in the family room, I opened a can of beer and took the first sip.

Oh my, it tastes so bad, how do people drink six to twelve cans of it? I guess it's an acquired taste. How am I going to drink this? You're drinking this for medicinal purpose and not for fun, I told my self sternly, taking another sip. *Remember the pain from yesterday? If the stone doesn't come out on its own, you'll need surgical intervention. Do I want to go that route? No, I don't. Then drink the beer and flush this rock out of your system; anything to avoid surgery.*

I convinced myself and somehow, I drank a third of the can, reassuring myself that it was a medicine, not a leisure drink. Suddenly I felt light headed and nauseous, and beads of fine sweat appeared on my forehead. I was going to get sick.

I looked Manju in the eyes. "I don't feel good."

"What's happening?" She glanced at the can in my hand.

"I feel nauseous and dizzy."

"You don't listen!" And then she yanked the can of beer from my hand and said, "Why do you do crazy things? You have never taken an alcoholic drink. You don't need this. I am going to throw all this away. Now lie down." I lay on the sofa for a good thirty minutes, and slowly started feeling better. I decided that never again would I indulge in alcohol.

The next day I narrated the events of the past few of days to a friend. He said, "I read in a health journal that chamomile tea is helpful for kidney stones. It relaxes the ureter. Try it and let me know if it works." I was willing to try anything to avoid surgery or go through the agonizing pain.

I went over to GNC store and got a packet of chamomile tea, and took it back to my office and asked my office manager Barbara to fix me a pot of tea. I drank two cups of the tea and was on the third cup when I had the uncontrollable urge to urinate. I rushed to the bathroom. It was extremely painful until I saw the stone hitting the bottom of the toilet bowl with a 'plink'. What an instant relief it was. Thank God the sucker was out.

The kidney stone was an experience of pain I will never forget, and remains vivid in my memory. In comparison, the knee surgery was uneventful. What had changed? In 1988, I was completely entrenched in the mundane world, whereas in 2005; I surrendered to God on the operating table and took refuge under His wings.

The recovery was magical, and it made a believer out of me.

Chapter 28

FIRST DAY AT THE OFFICE

In my mind I was comparing the two events of the kidney stone in 1988 and the knee surgery last week, when the elevator door opened on the fourth floor in front of my office. I walked into my office and said "Good morning."

My secretary and filing clerk just looked at me without speaking, amazed. Obviously they were expecting me to hobble in on crutches, and there I was, walking in as if nothing had happened. I said "Good morning" again. They replied in unison "Good morning", and then "How are you feeling?"

"I'm fine."

"How did the surgery go?" They were standing with their eyes wide open, hands on their cheeks, looking at me in shock.

"It went very well. See, I'm walking. I've been blessed. Thanks for asking."

I wondered what they were thinking. *Was Dr. B on vacation or did he really have surgery?* Jackie asked "Are you okay, Dr. B? We expected you with crutches and a big bandage on your knee. You look great."

"I feel great. I have no pain. With God's Grace, I'm walking without any discomfort."

I walked into my personal office at the end of the hall, put on my white coat and stethoscope and prepared myself to see patients. Jackie came in to check on me and I asked her to sit down. "I have something to tell you."

She looked at me, still perplexed. "Dr. B, really, you have no pain?"

"Yes Jackie, I have absolutely no pain, and I have been pain free since my surgery."

"This is unbelievable."

"God touched my knee on Tuesday. I am Healed."

She looked at me with a shadow of doubt.

"I had a conversation with God while I lay on the operating table. Not just a one-sided conversation, but a two-sided one. He replied and blessed me." She looked at me astonished, with eyes wide open. She stayed quiet as if wondering what part of my statement to believe and what not to believe. I interrupted her thoughts with my enthusiasm, "I'm not joking. I did have a conversation with God. He called me 'Son'. He was by my side. I surrendered to His will and I am healed. I have had no pain."

She was still bewildered at my excitement. I could see her wondering, *Is this the same Dr. B I have known for the past eight years talking to me? What happened to him?*

"Jackie, I have witnessed the Power of faith. Do you believe in God and His magic?"

Finally, she found her voice and replied, "Yes! I do." But I saw a glimpse of skepticism still lurking in her eyes. "Dr. B, I am so glad you are feeling better. It's good to see you back in the office. Don't push your self today. If you need anything, let me know."

I sat there for a few minutes to thank God again for His blessings, and went into the exam room to start my routine of seeing patients.

The first patient Mr. Sam Carter and his wife Nina were in the exam room waiting for me. This couple is very religious and they are devout Christians. They belong to a local church and have friends who also come to our practice. They have endured serious health issues over the years. Mrs. Carter had cancer of the kidney. She underwent Nephrectomy—removal of the kidney. Through this whole ordeal, Mr. and Mrs. Carter always talked about God and their faith. They were concerned but graciously accepted everything that happened to them as God's will. I have always seen them smiling and happy. After I entered the exam room; they surveyed my posture, and then looked at my knee, clearly expecting me to need crutches.

Surprised as they were, they inquired about my surgery, and I related the same story to them, and how I had been blessed and healed. I told them the whole experience. I knew they were people of faith and would believe my story. I had several discussions with them about medical issues over the years, but not on faith and healing.

"Praise the Lord", she said, "I am so happy to see you're feeling better."

It was reassuring to talk to somebody who connected with me and understood my faith. As they were walking out, they looked at me and said "What a miracle." I smiled and went to the next exam room to see another patient.

My last patient of the day was scheduled for exercise treadmill test. He was hooked up to the EKG monitor and the treadmill, waiting for me. I walked in to the procedure room. He turned and looked at me, surprised. "Dr B, I thought you had knee surgery last week? How are you feeling"?

"I'm fine" I said. "See, I'm navigating without any problem. I'm not ready to run on the treadmill yet, but I have been blessed. Thank God."

I could see that he was a bit upset. He had a similar surgery a few years ago, and was on crutches for over two weeks, and took painkillers for three weeks.

"How come you are healed in a short period of time?" He frowned, and I could see his jaw muscles tighten as he looked at me. "That's not right. I suffered so much with that stupid surgery."

"Every patient is different." I said, "Some heal quickly, while others take a few days. Some even take a few weeks or months." I wasn't sure whether I could talk to him about faith or not. Would he be receptive to this discussion? I couldn't resist and said, "Jim, you know, I was healed by faith in Almighty God. I completely surrendered to His Will. He touched me. There is no other explanation for this. Do you believe in God? Do you have faith?"

He was completely taken aback. *Dr. B, talking about faith and healing?* With some skepticism and then a flicker of self-doubt he said, "I know there is a God."

I said to him, "Surrendering to God's Will and having full faith is the key. You'll see for yourself what I am talking about. Let's start your test and see if your heart is healthy." His exercise test was normal. I reassured him and said "Jim, we'll continue our discussion on faith some other time." He thanked me and left the office.

After surgery my perspective changed about life, family and material possessions. I'd lost all interest in thoughts of material possessions. They weren't important any more. My body suddenly became very important. Every piece of its physiology, all the parts and its functions that I'd taken for granted all these years, now became precious. My family and loved ones were much more important than ever before. My work could wait. Suddenly, the time I could never get off from work was available to heal the damaged knee. Sickness made time available to me. I didn't have to think for a minute. Everything could wait.

I looked forward to coming back to the office and falling back into the routine. I was curious to find out if anyone was interested in listening to my story about what had happened to me in the hospital. As soon as I started to share it, everyone else had a story to tell me. They could care less about my surgery, because their story was much better and more interesting than mine. I was amazed. I always thought I had become a very important member of society, and everyone would miss me. Alas! The contrary was true. No one missed me. The world had been moving right along in my absence.

My experience on the operating table and the painless recovery since the operation made my faith steadfast, whereas earlier it had stood on shaky grounds. Repeatedly some strong force nudged me forward to tell others how it all happened. *Be bold, say it exactly how it happened. Don't be afraid.*

The fear of ridicule by others in society was overpowered by this juggernaut from within. I tried my best to suppress it and keep it close to my heart, but to no avail. It sat in me like a projectile, ready to be fired at any moment. Talking about this experience didn't satisfy my urge, and I felt a strong need to spread it all over the globe through writing. I was not an English or Literature major. On the contrary, I am a doctor. Language skills are marginal in the medical profession, but the more I wrote, the more I wanted to write.

Seeing patients, listening to them and helping them, gives me a great sense of professional satisfaction. On numerous occasions, I have witnessed patients getting better without any treatment. Those are moments of spiritual healing. The real fun starts after all my employees have left the office and I sit back and mull over the happenings of the day. Then I feel the presence of the Lord more than ever. There is no one around; just the Dear Lord and myself, in a perfect setting for solace and peace.

I look outside the window. The Sun is setting in the western sky. The gleaming rays of the setting Sun pierce through the clouds and light up the sky in red, orange and violet colors, so soothing and yet so powerful, many clouds, many different forms of them, suspended in the air, and they remind me of the magical creation of Almighty God. I kneel down and thank the Lord for giving me the opportunity to witness His drama in the sky. Of course, I enjoy the show, but more important than that is my faith in the power of the controller behind all this. Suspended in the universe is a small planet Earth, on which I stand as a tiny particle, so humbled to see a fraction of his immense magnanimity.

My knee held up very well today, the first day back at work after the surgery. I had an appointment with my orthopedic surgeon the next day, and I looked forward to hearing what he would say about my knee. I picked up my briefcase and walked out of my office to the parking garage. I thanked God for His blessings and wondered what tomorrow would have in store for me.

In my heart, I felt a burning desire to help others in the same way I had been blessed.

Chapter 29

DYING SOUL

In the middle of the night on a Saturday I was called to the Emergency Room to admit a seriously ill patient who was dying. He was Dr. Carter's patient, but I was the doctor on call for the weekend, so I was going to meet the patient for the first time in the emergency room. While driving to the hospital, I started thinking about death, the last chapter of one's life. What happened in the end? What thoughts were going through that patient's mind? Did he have a family? How were they? *What do I need to say or do to make it easier for them?*

Dear Lord, I am witnessing a dying patient. I want to make his last journey peaceful and pain free with your help. Almighty, you are the controller of the beginning, the end and what ever is in between. Please help me to help the sick and be their companion through death and disease.

For fifteen minutes I prayed in the car until I reached the hospital, parked and entered the emergency room to see the patient. When I walked into the exam room, his wife and son were waiting for me.

Mr. Thomas had terminal gastrointestinal cancer. He had two tubes in his abdomen; one tube called the gastrostomy tube was in his stomach to relieve distention and the second tube was a jejunostomy, inserted in his small intestines to feed him.

"Hi! I am Dr. Bhushan" I introduced myself. "I'm covering for Dr. Carter. Mr. Thomas, how are you feeling?"

He had an oxygen mask on his face, and appeared thin and emaciated. His cheekbones were visible through the wasted muscles of his face. His eyes were sunken, set deep into the sockets, and the orbital area had lost its flesh. He was moaning, groaning and writhing in pain. He could barely open his eyes. His wife grimaced at each moan. As I walked to his bedside, she moved to the other side of his bed and held his hand. His son could not bear to see the pain and agony his dad was in. He would turn away momentarily and then come back and stand near his father's feet.

"Dad, is the painkiller working yet?"

"No . . . Oh . . . my stomach hurts." Through one corner of his eyes, he looked and whispered in a low raspy voice, "Thanks, Dr. B for coming to see me at this

0

time. The Lord has blessed me in so many ways. Oh! Oh! Um uh! Mm. My stomach hurts Dr. B. Can you give me something for the pain?"

"Yes, Mr. Thomas, I will get you some more pain killer right away." I briskly walked over to the nursing station and asked the nurse to give Mr. Thomas intravenous narcotic pain medication. As I stood by his gurney, the distress of his pain was visible.

A few minutes later I came back to his room after reviewing his chart. "Mr. Thomas, how are you feeling? Is the pain any better?"

"Not a whole lot better, Dr. B," he said. "Thank you so much for coming. I am dying, Dr. B." Turning to his wife, he said with remorse, "Honey, I'm dying. It's true. Please let me go." And then back to me, "Dr. B please put me to sleep. The Lord has blessed me with sixty years of life, a wonderful family, a loving wife and two great sons."

I knew Mr. Thomas was suffering, and I wanted to relieve his pain right away. I wanted to hold his hand tight and tell him, 'Mr. Thomas, I will help you go to sleep right away with an extra dose of painkiller.' I wanted to ease his pain any way I could, but I couldn't help him die. We have come a long way in the last twenty-five years in caring for terminally ill patients, but euthanasia is not an acceptable mode of treatment, even in terminally ill patients. We cannot play God.

His every moan pierced my heart. His shallow breath seemed to suck the air out of my lungs, and his pale clammy face drained energy out of my body. I felt as if I were withering away right there with him. There was no one who could help him. My hands were tied. Other than the painkillers, I could not do anything else.

As a doctor, I'm supposed to heal the sick and take pain and suffering away, but I could do very little for this dying man. *This is a tragedy, but I am going to help him any way I can. Within the confines of this room I am going to jump over the limits of my profession as a doctor and become his friend here tonight.* I decided not to leave him until he felt better. I held his hand, gave him more painkillers and whispered in his ear, "Mr. Thomas, I am here with you. I am not going to leave and I will do whatever is in my power to take your pain away." Death was inevitable in his case, but to see him suffer in pain felt unbearable and inhumane. I didn't want to kill him with a narcotic overdose, but his suffering had to be relieved. I had to do something.

He looked at me; a tiny glimpse of smile barely visible through the oxygen mask, yet it resonated like bright laughter in my soul. I had connected with him not just as a doctor, but also as a friend. Now, I knew his pain would come under control as I had gained access to his heart through compassion and concern. His smile was all I was waiting for. He closed his eyes and tried to rest. A few minutes later, what seemed to be a lifetime, the painkillers finally worked and he opened his eyes.

"Honey, I am sorry to leave you." he said to his wife. "Will you forgive me?" She looked at him, tears rolling down her cheeks. She held his hand with one hand and slowly caressed his forehead and his hair. With a sob she said, "We had a wonderful marriage. We had so many great years together. I will miss you, dear. But I can't see you suffer like this. Don't worry about us." His son, standing on the other side of the stretcher broke down and said "Dad, I love you."

"I'm sorry I can't spend more time with you guys."

"You've been a great dad. Don't say that, Dad. Please."

"Take care of your mom when I'm gone."

He turned to me and said, "The Lord has blessed me with such a great, loving and wonderful family, Dr. B." His voice choked, and I knew his eyes would have filled with tears if the cancer hadn't sucked all the water from them. I stood there holding his other hand with the rest of his family, and admired this dying soul. He was thanking everyone so humbly; in spite of the immense pain he must have felt so close to death. He was teaching me about the meaning of life, our blessings, love and family. He was not afraid of death or the painful journey he was enduring, but he was concerned about others, especially the family he was leaving behind. I had not done much for him. I just happened to be the doctor on call for our group, but he was thanking me again and again. I wanted to be the one thanking him for showing me how to live through death. Slowly he drifted into sleep. The pain medication had temporarily alleviated his suffering.

He was transferred to the intensive care unit from the emergency room, sedated and pain free, at least for the moment. I left the emergency room after he was comfortable. It was two in the morning by the time I left the hospital to go home. In the car, I could not get over what I had just witnessed in the emergency room for the past two hours. A dying man in agony, not concerned about his illness, not concerned about his tragedy, but worried about everyone else, counting his blessings, thanking everyone around him. Here I saw a man of God, spreading God's word, not by living but through his death. I saw death looming over him, yet he was free and connected to the Lord with a smile on his face.

Every time I see a dying patient and experience death, it takes an emotional toll on me, and it chips away a part of me. Either I can be a distant professional, or I can become the patient's friendly doctor. I believe I am in the latter group. I feel their pain. I suffer as they suffer. When I see a family lose a loved one, it seems as if I am losing someone close to me. On many occasions, my eyes fill with grief and I have to work hard to hold back. It is difficult at times, and I cry with them. I want to be strong and not let my emotions come in the middle of patient care, but I am human. It happens. It may appear ridiculous to some, but to me it feels normal. I was there with them, as a part of the family, supporting them medically and emotionally when they needed it the most.

We are all God's children. It is a big family under one banner. To help others in pain makes me feel closer to God.

The next day, I went to see Mr. Thomas in the Intensive Care Unit. "Mr. Thomas, how are you feeling? Is your abdominal pain any better?"

"It's a little better." He wanted to talk to me in person about his terminal care with no one around. "I am dying Dr. B. Please put me on a morphine drip. Please put me to sleep. I cannot take this pain any more. I can't see my family suffer with me."

"Mr. Thomas, I want to discuss this with your family. Would you have any objection to it?"

"No, Dr. B, my wife is outside. You can bring her in."

I walked over to the nursing station and asked the nurse to bring Mrs. Thomas into the room. The nurse came back with his wife.

"Mrs. Thomas, did you stay with Mr. Thomas here in the ICU last night? How was he?"

"He was in pain off and on. My son was here too. We took turns."

Looking at Mr. Thomas, I said, "Mrs. Thomas, your husband has requested a continuous intravenous infusion of morphine so he can die peacefully."

"Is that what you wish, honey?" she asked him sadly.

"Yeah! Oh, oh, mm, my stomach hurts."

She looked directly at him. "If you want to wait for Dr. Carter, he'll be back in the morning. You can decide with him." She paused; clearly wanting to delay the process, then asked to me, "What do you think, Dr. B?"

"Mr. Thomas, you seem to be better compared to last night in the emergency room. We can try increasing your pain killers to see if that works, before putting you on a continuous infusion of morphine."

"Dr. B, I get relief for a short while and then the pain comes back with a vengeance."

"Let's see how it works for you with an increased dosage of painkillers. In the mean time, you and your family can decide what you want us to do. I'll discuss your request with Dr. Carter. He knows you and your condition much better than I do. He'll be back tomorrow morning to see you."

"That sounds reasonable," his wife said to him.

"Thanks Dr. B, for all your help."

"I don't want you to suffer, Mr. Thomas. I'm here to help you. I've left instructions in your record for the nursing staff to give you additional pain medication whenever you need it." I left the ICU to finish my rounds at the hospital.

Mr. Carter stayed in the hospital for thirteen days. I saw him a couple of times during those days when I was covering for Dr. Carter. His condition continued to deteriorate, though the pain was kept under control with a heavy dose of pain killers.

Mr. Thomas was discharged under the care of Hospice. I learnt through Dr. Carter that Mr. Thomas passed away peacefully at home surrounded by his wife and two sons a week later.

Chapter 30

SHORTCOMINGS

Tuesday morning, a week after my surgery, I had an appointment with Dr. Kaplan at 10:00 AM. I parked my car and walked to his office, signed in at the front desk and sat down in the waiting room. The large aquarium on the wall caught my attention again. The multicolored fish seemed to enjoy the surroundings; one moment they were stationary, the next they took a sharp turn and swiftly swam away, as if playing with each other. The receptionist at the front desk informed me that Dr. Kaplan was running late due to an emergency at the hospital earlier in the morning.

One patient in the waiting room asked someone next to her, "How long have you been waiting?" She replied "one hour", at which she exclaimed, "My day is shot, anyway, but he is a good doctor." The other patient said, "My neighbor referred me to Dr. Kaplan. He's very good."

I picked up an automobile magazine and was browsing through it when I saw another patient walk in with crutches, and thought to myself: *This could be me.*

Why have I been given this easy, painless recovery? Is Almighty God holding my hand and guiding me in a new direction? Maybe I've been forgiven for all the sins I've committed, Maybe I've escaped this time. I'd better start doing the right things.

I decided to make a list of all my shortcomings. When I finished, my list was so long I felt ashamed. *How did it get so long?*

The first item on my list was anger. I knew I had an issue with anger, and found it hard to let it go. It always took me a while to cool off. When I had to blow off steam, I didn't hurt anyone physically, but I knew I inflicted heavy damage emotionally.

I thought about the time a few months earlier, when Manju was going grocery shopping. I was in my study working when I heard a loud bang in the garage. When I ran out to see what happened, I saw Manju standing next to the bent garage door. Apparently, she had not opened the garage door and backed our beautiful new car into it.

She stood there looking scared and said, "I hit the garage door with my bumper. I'm sorry."

A volcano of anger erupted in me. "How can you be so stupid?" I screamed at her, unable to control myself and ran to look at the rear bumper of my beautiful black car. There was a tiny area on the bumper where the paint had chipped off, barely visible to the naked eye from ten feet away. The garage door had a minor concave indentation on it. I stood there for a few seconds, inspecting the damage that was so miniscule and yet it agitated me until I felt completely out of control. I knelt on the floor and bent down to analyze the damage. It was a small blemish.

After a while, I looked up, feeling the wild impulse to scream at her, but I was paralyzed with anger.

Manju stood there trembling, close to tears, repeating over and over, "I am sorry."

Eventually, I calmed myself and put my hand on her shoulder and said, "Don't worry, it's all right" even though the anger inside me was still going full throttle, ready to combust. The anger wasn't satisfied, and wanted to continue the verbal abuse and inflict more emotional and mental torture on her. For another hour the battle raged in my brain.

Over the past years my anger has been the biggest hurdle for me to cross, even after multiple attempts to control it. I still could not extinguish the fire inside.

But one episode in the operating room changed me. When I surrendered myself to God, I knew I had to surrender my anger too.

Let me hope it's not too late to start over. No, it's never too late. I can start any time. Now is as good a time as any to start. Once I made the list, I studied it and read it out loud to myself. The best time was in the morning, before I began my day. I pasted the list of my shortcomings on the mirror, and told myself, 'Try to be a better person'.

My flaws were many. I wanted everything to be perfect, and found too many faults with others. I resolved to work on controlling my anger. I knew it wasn't out of control, but it was an internal problem as well as an external flaw. Internally, no one could see it, but it damaged my well-being. It could cause a deadly heart attack. Externally, it was visible to the people around me and I knew it made them uncomfortable.

I resolved to appreciate others as God's children and accept whatever happened around me as God's Will. I wasn't perfect. How could I expect others to be perfect? Usually anger came after something that had already happened. The damage was done, and the event was already in the past. It was history, so getting angry wasn't going to change it. *The best thing is to accept it and move on.*

One night, a funny thing happened. I was sitting in my own thoughts, analyzing my faults when I burst out laughing so loud that Manju called from the other room, "What's going on?"

"Oh! It's nothing" I said

"Then why are you laughing so loud?"

"I'm laughing at my own stupidity."

"Really! I thought you were perfect."

"Perfect! Me? It's taken me fifty three years to realize how stupid I've been."

"Don't worry," she replied. "It's never too late. I'm glad you finally realized it. I still love you."

"I love you too."

There are so many stupidities. The biggest one was being unable to forgive and forget. I carried a baggage of events which occurred in my past with family, some so trivial, and yet they stayed in my subconscious and at times came to the forefront and completely preoccupied my brain. As I started shedding my grudges, like a serpent sheds scaly skin, it became a new beginning for me. It was difficult initially as these thoughts would come roaring back and stir up my mind. They were stealthy, aiming for revenge and leaving me with a mental anguish and exhaustion. I wasted an unimaginable amount of time and energy just pondering what I should have said or done in the past.

Now I had a much better mental outlook, with no internal agitation. Forgiveness became one of my pillars of strength, and I stood on it firmly, with no fear of an emotional tumble. Surrendering to God's will yielded this power and built an inner fortitude.

The nurse called my name and asked me to follow her. I was so deep in the glory of God that I had forgotten where I was. I put the magazine down, got up and walked to the door, which led to the examination room.

"Hello, I'm Kathy. I'm Dr. Kaplan's nurse today. How are you feeling? How is the pain in your knee?"

"There is no pain."

"Are you able to walk without tightness or stiffness?"

"Yes, there is no restriction, it feels great."

"Is there any swelling?"

"I don't think so. Dr. Kaplan will be opening the bandage today" At that answer, she looked in the chart to see when exactly I had the surgery.

"Dr. Kaplan did a remarkable job." I smiled to myself because I knew what had happened in the operating room.

She gave me a gown to change into and said, "Dr. Kaplan will be in shortly."

As I sat in the tiny exam room, my mind began working again. *Dr. Kaplan will be proud of me for doing so well.*

Wait a moment; why would he be proud of me? I haven't done a thing. He'll be proud of his work. He knows he's the one who operated on my knee—I'm only a patient. Stay quiet and listen to what Dr. Kaplan has to say. He should be the one to enjoy his success. He worked hard to operate on me.

But, how can he take credit for this? God came and touched my knee.

I can't say this to Dr. Kaplan. He'll be offended.

He shouldn't mind if he believes in God and has faith.

Maybe I should stay quiet.

On the other hand, maybe I'll tell Dr. Kaplan.

The tug of war continued in my mind until the door opened and Dr. Kaplan walked in with a smile. We shook hands and he sat down on the stool.

"So how's the knee?"

"Tom, I feel fine. I have no pain. I'm navigating without any problems."

"Really? That's great. Can you get on the exam table, Raj? Let me examine your knee."

He took the bandage off and examined the wound. "This looks beautiful; hardly any swelling. The three areas where the holes were drilled looked clean and dry." He applied pressure on the wounds to see if they were tender. "Maybe the bottom one has a little swelling." He maneuvered the joint, checked the flexion and extension. "Looks good." He looked into my eyes and said, "I'm really pleased with the progress." Then he proceeded to take out the stitches from the three wounds and applied Band-Aids to them.

"You should go and see the physical therapist, Kelly, for strengthening and rehabilitation. She'll recommend some exercises."

"Tom, Do I really need physical therapy? I feel fine."

"It will speed up your recovery," he said. "I'll give you a referral for physical therapy, and I'd like you to see Kelly."

"When do I have a follow-up with you, Tom?"

"Follow up in two weeks. You're doing very well."

I debated whether or not I should talk about the episode in the operating room, but the urge to share my experience made it extremely difficult for me to avoid talking about God. I was going to burst with the spiritual commotion inside me. I couldn't keep it in me. It was too powerful.

"Tom, God came to the OR in your form to heal me. He was right there and I had a conversation with Him. He called me 'son', and He gave me love and reassurance, Tom. I'm not joking. It's true." I relayed the whole experience to him without leaving anything out.

Dr. Kaplan paused and looked at me for a moment in a very doubtful manner. Obviously, he could not believe what I was saying.

I continued, "I'm not kidding, Tom. That's exactly how it was. I haven't had any pain or discomfort since I left the operating room. I even had to open the bandages and look at the wound to confirm that I had the surgery. There has been no pain whatsoever."

"Really, are you serious?"

"Yes, I'm serious. I haven't taken the painkillers you prescribed for me. Not even one. Believe it or not, not even a Tylenol." I studied his face for a moment before I spoke again. "Tom, do you believe what I've just described to you? Do you have faith in Almighty God and the power of healing?"

He was completely baffled by my question. He grinned and opened his eyes wide. Then he was quiet for a moment. He opened his mouth to say something and then paused as if he could not decide what to say. He looked at me again, clearly unable to comprehend what I had told him. He shook his head and looked up towards the ceiling and smiled, "You really have had no pain."

"Yes! Tom, I am not making it up."

He was quiet for a moment and then said, "A few years back, I had a similar experience with a very sick patient. Maybe it's true. Miracles do happen sometimes." I saw a degree of uncertainty in his eyes that changed to a tranquil look of faith.

Dr. Kaplan told me about his patient who healed when medical science thought otherwise. I could see he felt better after talking about it. I could see his faith and belief deepening. He wished me well, then suggested that I continue strengthening exercises, and see him if needed.

I left Dr Kaplan's office, very happy for two reasons. First, of course was the selfish one that my knee was healing well, but the second one was more important to me, and that was because I'd been able to talk to a colleague about God and faith, for the first time in the twenty five years I have been practicing medicine. To my utmost surprise, there was some degree of acceptance at the end of our conversation. I was bubbling with joy because of that achievement. I felt I was on the right course, and I wasn't afraid to talk about it. The door had opened for me to walk through to the other side. The spiritual side had taken precedence over medical science.

I took the prescription for physical therapy and scheduled the appointment with Kelly for the following day. By now I was fully engaged in conversation with God, and continued to savor His Grace and His blessings. The more I pondered, the more it became clearer. His Grace was visible in every one around me.

Chapter 31

ATHEIST

Mrs. Tillman, a dear patient of mine, came to see me for abdominal pain in the summer of 2006. Somehow the discussion came to the subject of God.

She said, "Dr. B, my dad is an atheist. He doesn't believe in God and God's creation. I don't believe in God either. We're here on this earth on our own. We bear the consequences of our own actions. No one is here to look after us. Really, no one knows where we come from and where we go."

I was taken aback. How could she say that? I was upset and a little angry at her declaration that there was no God. I thought about how I might convince her when I'd had my own doubts about Him just a short while ago. I hadn't seen God, but I believed in Him. Now I had faith.

I knew I had to respect her opinion. Maintaining my composure, I said, "Mrs. Tillman, you're right, and I appreciate hearing your point of view. It's an interesting discussion. Perhaps one day we'll discuss it further."

She went through extensive testing, including blood tests, sonogram and CAT scans. All her tests were normal. She was referred to a gastroenterologist for a second opinion. His conclusion was abdominal pain secondary to irritable bowel syndrome. He prescribed medications, but she had no relief. She was reevaluated and the consensus was that she might have gall bladder disease. She came again to see me and wanted my advice about having gall bladder surgery.

I said, "Mrs. Tillman, my clinical evaluation is consistent with gall bladder problem, and I think you should get it removed."

She seemed to accept my answer, but still had questions. "Dr. B, are you sure it's my gall bladder?"

"I'm not one hundred percent sure, but your symptoms point towards chronic gall bladder inflammation."

"Will surgery relieve my abdominal pain?"

"Yes! It will, if they find inflammation in your gall bladder."

"Is it a simple operation? How long does it take?"

"It's done laparoscopically; Mrs. Tillman. It should take about an hour. You should ask the surgeon these questions. They deal with this everyday."

"What is a Laparoscopic procedure, Dr. B?"

"Instead of a conventional incision, the surgeon operates through three holes, one at the belly button, and two on the right upper abdomen. It is done through a laparoscope. You go home the same day and the recovery is much faster."

"Are there any long term ill effects of this surgery?"

"A small percentage of patients have fat intolerance and diarrhea, but it's easily manageable."

"Let me think about it and talk to my husband. Thank you so much for explaining all this to me. Please give me the name and telephone number of the surgeon and I'll schedule an appointment."

During our conversation, the discussion of God and faith came up again. She asked me, "Dr. B, do you really believe in God?"

I told her, "I think I do. Who else is there to believe?" She smiled and said, "I grew up in a family of Atheists, and I feel there is no God. Dr. B, I trust you. If you feel removing the gall bladder will help my symptoms, I'll schedule the surgery."

She underwent Cholecystectomy—gall bladder removal. Two weeks after the surgery, she came to see me. I entered the exam room and asked her, "How are you feeling?"

"I feel great. I have no abdominal pain. Thank God for your persistence and sending me for surgery." I was astonished to hear her say 'Thank God.'

Then she said "Really, thank God I got the gall bladder removed."

I looked at her and asked, "Do you realize what you just said? You said 'Thank God' two times. You said you'd never believed in God and yet, you just said, 'Thank God'."

She was shocked. "Dr. B, you're right. I did say, 'Thank God'. Maybe I believe in God after all, but I hadn't realized it. Dr. B, Thank you so much for reminding me of what I just said."

Here was a woman who'd been an Atheist for fifty years, who suddenly became aware of God's existence through her sickness. It fascinated me to see a new believer in God. My faith was confirmed again with God's Grace that day.

I saw a hint of faith in her throughout our conversation about her illness. She was not saddened, but rather elated by the challenge of her illness and the possibility that God had helped her. Maybe there was a seed in her which lay dormant for all these years and her sickness became the vehicle to help it sprout. Her demeanor became cheerful. I felt as if she found something she had lost a long time back. Somehow, she appeared happier than before. At least, that is what I perceived during her subsequent visits. To me, this tiny glimpse of hope hidden in her newfound faith helped me in my pursuit of belief.

I called Mrs. Tillman recently and we talked for a while. I was curious as to how her faith was progressing. She was excited to hear from me. The first thing she said, "Dr. B. Guess what—I am reading a book right now on faith from The Oprah book club."

"Really! That's great."

"Since my last visit to your office six months back, we've gone to the temple three times as a family. You know, Dr. B, we hadn't visited the temple once in the last six years since we moved to the United States."

As she talked, I could hear and feel the new found energy of faith in her. She sounded content, thrilled about the change in her life style. Even though she still had adversity in her life, she had hope. She was changing and leaning more towards faith and belief.

"I know you're busy, but I would love to come over, sit down and talk to you more about faith whenever you have time," she said.

"Please do come and we'll talk."

"Dr. B, I'm glad you called today. Thank you."

Chapter 32

PHYSICAL THERAPY

My scheduled appointment for physical therapy was with Kelly, the same therapist who had helped me with my back a few months ago. I signed in the book on the reception counter, grabbed a hard candy from the candy jar and sat down to wait for my appointment. It was a small waiting room, about eight feet by twelve feet with six burgundy vinyl chairs lined against the wall, and two small end tables topped with assorted magazines.

The place was busy with patients moving in and out, and many of them had crutches, splints or braces. Here I was, sitting with my original package of limbs. I listened to a gentleman who had had knee surgery three months earlier, was still undergoing physical therapy, and was in pain most of the time. I kept absolutely quiet.

There was no reason to brag about my quick, painless recovery—he might take it the wrong way. It was a humbling experience. Someone who had to endure pain and suffering wouldn't want to listen to my story of miraculous healing.

Still, my inner voice urged me to speak to others and persuade them of the power of faith, surrender and healing. I was not looking for fame, and I didn't want any special treatment. I was just like anyone else out there. Even though I was convinced of this mortal world's problems, I felt guided by this force to make others aware of this invisible power that was so willing to help others in need and despair. This force would not let me rest until I talked about it whenever I could. The more I tried to suppress it or trap it in me, the more I felt uneasy. I had to let it out.

As I looked at this middle-aged man going through therapy for so long, I felt sad. I wanted to talk to him about God, faith and patience. But how would he respond? *Will he be upset, or get mad at me, and tell me to shut up?* Talking to a stranger about this could backfire. Particularly one who had been suffering for a while. Their faith had really been put to the test. I decided to keep it to myself for now and prayed for his healing.

Kelly came to the waiting room and took me to the therapy area. I sat down on the chair in the exam room.

"Hi, Dr. B, What are you doing here?"

"I had my knee operated on last Tuesday by Dr. Kaplan. I had a torn meniscus that had started bothering me quite a bit." Smiling, I added, "You know how it is after you turn fifty—you start to fall apart. But, then, you wouldn't know that, you're too young for that."

She just smiled back and said, "Dr. B, you are not old. You're only fifty two years young."

"I guess you're right. It could be worse."

"Did you see Dr. Kaplan? What did he say?"

"He said that my knee is healing very well."

"That's wonderful. Did he give you a prescription for therapy?"

"Yes, he did. Here it is."

"Can you get on the exam table?" she asked.

"Sure," I said and got on the table.

She looked at the knee. "Hardly any swelling. When did you say you had the operation?"

"Last Tuesday."

She was obviously surprised to see the strength and flexibility of my knee. As she measured the range of motion and compared the two legs, she suddenly exclaimed, "Dr. B, there is only five degree difference between the right and the left knee. You will not need any therapy. All you need is some strengthening." I listened to all that she had to say and counted my blessings. She took me to the weight bearing/strengthening area of the room and showed me leg presses, balance exercises and the weights. I learned all the techniques for home exercise, then thanked her for her time and input and walked out of the physical therapy suite.

It was difficult for me to accept a painless recovery. Scientifically or medically, there has to be pain, swelling and diminished range of motion. But it was not there. So many patients have operations every day. I see them in pain, distress and sometimes in sheer agony, requiring large amounts of painkillers.

Here I am walking as if nothing has happened to me. This can be possible only with divine intervention. Maybe this is the last reminder from Almighty God. May be He wants me to change the direction and course of my life. Maybe He is opening a new door for me. Maybe, my faith had to take this giant leap. I cannot ignore this. My calling has come and I have to remember this every day of my busy, hectic life.

With God's Grace, I did not need any more physical therapy.

Chapter 33

MAN FROM GREECE

A few months back, I admitted a patient to the hospital with severe back problems from a herniated disc, and he was scheduled for surgery. This gentleman came from Greece with his wife to have the operation at the hospital. He suffered from other medical conditions for which he had brought medications with him. On the day of his admission to the hospital, his son brought the bag of medications for us to review. Prior to his operation, my nurse practitioner Opal and I looked at all his medications while finishing up his admission record. He underwent the surgery the next day and was transferred to another floor in the hospital for post op care. The day after the surgery, the patient and his wife inquired about the bag containing all his medicines. Usually, the articles accompany the patient during a transfer, but the medication bag apparently was misplaced.

When I went to see him at the hospital, he said, "Dr. B, I had five months of pills in that bag. These medicines are very expensive in the U.S. What am I going to do?" I could see he was getting worried and flushed with anxiety about all this.

"Mr. Peters, Please don't worry. We'll try to locate the medicine bag you brought with you from Greece. I know the medicines are expensive here in the U.S. Let's see what we can do."

His wife stood next to his bed, hands folded, looking worried. She asked in her thick Greek accent, "Doctor, will you look for the bag yourself? Will you find it?"

"I'll do my best. Please have faith."

They exchanged some words in Greek that I didn't understand, but could make out that they were less enthusiastic about the successful back surgery and more worried about the loss of the brown paper bag containing the pills for his medical ailments, and the expense associated with replacing it.

I tried to reassure them, but to no avail. "Mr. Peters, we'll try to get some samples from the office and if worse come to worst, we'll replace those medicines."

"No, no, Dr. B. I don't want you to do that." But I could see he was upset. I told him that I would go back to the floor where he was originally admitted and search for them myself. Opal and I walked out of his room.

I looked at her and asked, "Do you have faith?"

She said "Yes."

"We'll find the bag" I said. "I have faith." We went to the floor where he was initially admitted.

Opal said, "I hope we find it."

"Not hope. We will find it."

As we arrived at the nursing station, two nurses greeted us and said, "Dr. B, you're making early rounds today."

I said, "Pam, we admitted Mr. Peters here two days ago, and there was a brown paper bag with three different medications in it. Have you seen it?"

She smiled and said, "Its right here, Dr. B. It was sitting at the nursing station for a while. I wasn't certain who it belonged to. So I just put it in the back, hoping somebody would come looking for it."

Opal was shocked. In a big hospital, it's very easy for things to get misplaced, particularly, a brown paper bag with no name on it. We both looked at each other and thanked God.

"Dr. B, this is amazing!"

"Yes, it is."

I had faith the bag would be there. We took the bag back to Mr. Peters' room and gave it to his wife. They were so happy to see the medicine bag and repeatedly thanked God. A few years ago it might have seemed like a coincidence to me, but now I knew the magic of faith and how it worked in mysterious ways. The power of belief and faith were visible in everything, no matter how big or small, that was happening in my life. All I had to do was look for them. These spiritual raptures helped me climb the ladder of faith.

Chapter 34

REHABILITATION

My follow-up visit with Dr. Kaplan had gone well. He had examined me thoroughly and checked the range of motion of the operated knee, when he said, "This is as good as your right knee."

Excited with the news, I asked, "When can I run again?"

"Well, let us see. When you're able to hop on your left leg, you'll be ready to run."

"I guess that's my goal. I'll work towards that."

"Just continue on the strengthening exercises Kelly recommended. Those will get you moving quickly."

I was listening very carefully to his advice. I was focused on full rehabilitation. Faith and complete surrender had become the two wheels of my disabled chariot, and the Lord was the charioteer of this damaged knee. Full recovery was not far from my mind. I had faith because of the miracles I had seen so far, and I was determined to reach my goal.

I came home and discussed my visit with Dr. Kaplan and the therapist with Manju. She was happy to learn the outcome of my visits. I had to do my homework now; and start the rehabilitation of my knee. There were two options, to either go to the gym or bring it home. We had purchased a treadmill and an elliptical a couple of years before. What I needed now was a leg press machine and a stationary bike. The leg press machine strengthens the quadriceps and hamstrings, the big muscles of the thigh, which control the knee joint. The stationary bike would give me non-impact mobility and flexibility. We decided to buy the home gym and the stationary bike during Christmas holidays and create a nice gym/physical therapy center in our basement. The TV and exercise music motivated me to get in a mood to exercise. Alex and Rita took care of that, since the younger generation is more in tune with electronics and music.

After all the systems were in place, I began religiously working out an hour at a time, three to four times a week. I committed myself to get the knee back in shape. In three weeks, I was able to balance on my operated leg. Maneuvering on the steps was not difficult, though jumping on my left leg was still not possible, and that was my goal. I noticed significant improvement in six weeks, when I started testing myself on the treadmill with a light jog for couple of minutes. I didn't want to overdo, but I was eager to know how I was doing.

During the eighth week, the signs of recovery became clearly visible. I could hop for the first time in many months with no pain. From the day of the surgery until now, I had not taken even one painkiller tablet, aspirin or Tylenol.

I would finish my routine and look outside in the back yard. There was a mammoth oak tree at least two hundred years old, with a trunk over three feet in diameter, and over two hundred feet tall. It stood majestically between the other smaller trees, like a parent guarding his children. It was struck by lightning a couple of years ago, and a third of its trunk at the top was sheared off. Every time I looked at that tree, my faith in God took another leap. It reminded me that faith would keep me standing tall through all adversities.

Another day of my exercise routine went well. *Heartfelt Thanks! Dear Lord. I am so indebted to you for what you have done for me. I am afraid to even talk about it. Standing in the basement of my house, looking outside through the window, sunlight gleaming through denuded trees, a few puffy white clouds strolling across the beautiful blue sky, I admire your presence in my life. Lord, I witnessed your magic in the past. It seems so foolish to have ignored it over and over again. This time, you have given me another reminder by taking my pain and suffering. I have felt your touch, which has healed me; not only physically, but spiritually. I love you, My Lord. Please continue to guide me and keep me under your wings, so I can help others through your Power and Grace.*

Chapter 35

HOW TO FIND GOD

After two months of rehab, my knee felt great. Exercising four times a week really worked well. I was able to run, albeit at a slow pace. Two months before, walking was difficult, but at this point a light jog was a joy again.

It's late January and it's snowing. The ground is covered with a white blanket. The morning sun is rising above the horizon, the beam of light passing through the sparkling crystals of ice and snow tethered to the branches of the large oak tree. On the ground the glistening sheet of ice and snow is blinding from the accumulation of this drifting diamond dust during the night. The silence and solitude of winter is a gift to us from the Almighty God, the keeper of perfect celestial harmony. The stillness of long winter will not last long; time picks up its usual pace, days start to get longer and darkness will lose the battle again.

It's the first snow of the season. I watch the snowflakes coming down as they twist, turn and settle on the ground. The Sun will rise, the temperature will warm up and the frozen snowflake will melt. It will turn into water and seep into the ground, where it will meet and blend with a particle of soil. The particle of soil will keep absorbing the snowflakes, one on top of the other, patiently accommodating every one of these snowflakes. So friendly, so tolerant, just like the Almighty God. Oh! Lord Almighty, you exist in the small particle. The melting will continue until these tiny droplets coalesce together to form bigger ones and then they will unify to form a puddle of water, which in turn forms a stream. It will then flow into the river which ultimately finds its final resting place back in the ocean. My dear Lord pervades from the beginning as a snowflake to the end into the ocean and beyond, recreating the cycle again.

I am so preoccupied with my daily chores that I miss out on the Lord's Glory and His magical creation around me. I believe that the last two decades have taken me away from God. I am submerged in the technological gadgets. More and more information is available about everything except God.

Our entry on this planet is a very short journey from point A to point B. The arrival time is determined by time of conception, the duration of nine months and seven days from conception to birth. Doctors can predict our time of arrival, but the time of departure is hidden from us. There is always uncertainty. There is a lot of joy, happiness and excitement at the time of arrival. Anxiety, fear and grief take over at our departure. Physical transformation is the law of nature. It's like turning the page over. Birth to death and the time in between is all under the control of Almighty God. He is the knower of our full life cycle. Faith means total surrender in good and bad times. We are here on earth, on a testing ground, with a continuous barrage of problems incessantly pouring down on us. Life is nothing but trying to figure out how to stay afloat. Many times, it seems drowning is imminent, yet faith provides that last hope. Patience gives us that last glimmer and we continue to keep our head above water until we see the shore in the distance and inch by inch move closer to the safe grounds.

Unflinching faith is the only salvation for us.

It's 5:30 in the morning, six months after surgery. I walk down the steps to the basement to start my day with the morning workout. Dawn is breaking the veil of darkness. Blue sky is visible again, which appeared so dark a little while ago, except for the beautiful gibbous Moon and the stars twinkling so far away. A new day brings new hope. Another era begins today. The birds are chirping, feeding their young ones, busy with their routine, talking to each other with sounds and body language. Their chirping reminds me of yet another beautiful morning God has given to me.

The ground hog with her baby are busy finding their meal in the grass, digging away completely oblivious and at times raising their heads in fear of becoming a meal for another animal.

The baby deer is now a few days old. The white spots on his tan skin are still visible. He is clinging to his mama deer, which is busy grazing on the grass in the back yard. I see God in the tender new blades of grass. I see God in the ground, in the particle of soil from which the grass germinates. I see God in the birds and the animals around me. I see God in the trees, growing tall in the back yard. I see Him above in the sky. The sun is rising in the east. The beautiful radiant colors in the eastern sky are coming into the view. The dark black sky of the night past is changing shades from gray to light blue.

Oh Lord! I want to write about your magic, your creations and the drama around me. There are no limits, no boundaries to your Grace, blessings and bounteous gifts. Yesterday I was at the nursery to buy some flowers for the front yard. The pansies were so beautiful; the purples, the yellows and the double colored yellowish purple or purplish yellow. I stood and admired them and wondered how you created these flowers with beautiful colors. Each and every petal is different in shape and size. They are soft, smooth and delicate, yet can withstand wind, rain and sunshine, each with a unique color and shape of its own. From a distance, they appear identical with matching colors. On close inspection with naked eye, there are subtle differences, just like any other species of plant and animal. All look identical from a distance, but unique in their own ways.

My vision suddenly stops at my left knee. I see God in my knee. I see His touch on my knee. I see His healing power in my knee. I stand and walk. My ability to bear weight, bend and squat again feels like the old days. It feels good to be normal. Tomorrow is another busy day on the horizon. I hope I don't forget my dear Lord in this hectic life style of the twenty first century.

Chapter 36

FORWARD, BACKWARD *or* DEAD STOP

I have an office full of patients, and am getting calls every few minutes regarding a critically ill patient in the ICU at the hospital, and a patient in the emergency room waiting for me. My nurse has called in sick. The receptionist's son had an emergency appendectomy. The phone is ringing off the hook. My mother called me that she is not well. My son got hit on the head by a racket ball while playing and is dizzy in Boston. Manju calls in the middle of all this that the basement at home is flooded from the thunderstorms the night before. I stand in my office listening to all this. Today I have been beaten down in thirty minutes. There seems to be no end to the continuous barrage of problems attacking me from all directions. Life is so busy and it seems to be getting busier by the minute. All my energy is drained by unraveling the daily drama of life. I pause for a moment, put brakes on the information highway of my overloaded brain. My poor brain is inundated with all these problems and I'm completely confused. What to do?

Only one thing rescues me time and again. Remembering God and my faith provides me with a safe haven. I take a deep breath and look outside the window at the beautiful blue sky, the vast empty space way up there, which seems unmoved by all the confusion surrounding me. The sky gazes back at this world, completely oblivious to what goes on here in this office and my family at this moment. *Pause and let it unfold slowly Dr. B, don't rush it and don't chase it. Take your time. Calm down. Let the power out there handle everything here in your office, home and family. Let the provider of everything resolve this complicated mess.*

Certainly, things will resolve and get better. They always do. Rushing, getting angry or agitated will not change anything. *This shall pass too, Dr. B. I hope you have not forgotten the miracle of the last few months. I hope your faith is as strong as ever. Don't stumble now; let it be taken care of by the same entity that healed you.*

A new day begins. The next day starts with its own set of problems but all the staff is back in the office. The critical patient in ICU is doing much better. My son had to go to the emergency room in Boston for the head injury that he sustained while playing racket ball. He had an emergency CT scan that was normal. I breathed a sigh of relief. I called my nurse and prescribed her antibiotics for a sinus infection, then told her to rest for a day and drink lots of fluids. My receptionist called back from the hospital that her son was doing well after the appendectomy. Mom is feeling better. The leak in the basement turned out to be a minor problem. All these things that ganged up on me settled down just as quickly. One moment I felt completely surrounded and helpless, and the next moment, things were back to normal. My faith came to my rescue.

We all go through these problems. Sit back and slowly let it resolve itself. Tackle them one at a time. It didn't take long to resolve all the problems and difficult situations that seemed to choke me that day. What got me out of that mess was patience and faith. The day ended on a positive note. I look forward to tomorrow for what it brings and continue to climb the ladder of faith.

Chapter 37

I LOVE JESUS

My first patient on this Monday morning was a fifty three year old lady from Philippines, who wanted a complete physical examination. I had seen her in the office several times over the past eight years.

I walked into the exam room. "How are you Lori?"

"I'm fine, Dr. B."

"Do you have any physical concerns or ailments?"

"No! Dr. B, I feel fine. I'm here only for a physical."

"How is your family?"

"They are all doing fine," she smiled, "I am so blessed. I have a loving supportive husband and three wonderful kids. My job sometimes stresses me; you know how it is working in the post office."

"Yes, it can be stressful." I said, "But Lori, see how blessed you are. You're connecting people through the mail. You're helping people unknown to you all over the world. You're lucky. Let me examine you."

As I was going to put my stethoscope on her chest, she said, "Dr. B, I'm sorry I didn't change my clothes because I was rushing this morning. I was late for my appointment and I'm not looking nice today. I worked the night shift at the post office."

I paused and looked at her and said, "Lori, don't worry about it. Your outfit is fine. You're casual today. The outside appearance has little value compared to who we are inside."

"What do you mean, Dr. B?"

"I'm talking about the internal decoration. Your heart is made up of gold when you love God. Your outside will dazzle when the inside is illuminated with God's Love."

"Dr. B, do you love God so much?"

I was hesitant to talk about this with her. This was a private matter deep inside me. Could I discuss this with an outsider, and tell her about my feelings? Would she understand me? I couldn't share my level of faith and love for God with her. It was too precious and close, locked inside of me. *But if I'm not going to tell, how am I going to spread the word. I promised to the Almighty God on the operating table. I have to speak out. What if she laughs at me? She will not respect me as a doctor ever again. Doctors don't talk about faith and love for God. I'm uneasy with all this type of discussion. Maybe, I'll stay quiet and change the topic. But I can't. This is the only topic that interests me. I want everyone to listen to what I feel about God. I'll burst if I hold it all inside me. I witnessed it, experienced it. It's true. Go ahead and don't hesitate and say it loud. Be fearless. The Lord is guiding you. Go for it.*

"I don't know, maybe. I know for sure that He loves me so much that it makes me cry when I talk about Him."

She looked at my wet eyes and smiled.

"I don't know why, but it happens to me too. I cry too when I talk about God. God makes me feel good, Dr. B. I love Jesus and He sits inside me." She started crying saying those words. "You're right, Dr. B. He must love me too." We both stood there praising the Lord with our eyes wet, yet I knew both of us were happy and at peace.

I finished the examination, wished her well and walked out of the exam room. The rest of the day was busy as usual. The next day was Tuesday, the best day of the week, when I could go out for a walk in the morning and admire Lord's creation around me.

Surrendering to God's will has made life much better for me. I'm at peace with myself. To love God this way tickles my insides like nothing else. The joy it provides has no limits and the peace it gives is eternal.

My God is not superior to Jesus, Allah, Messiah, Buddha or any other Gods. There is only one God, the Supreme Power, and The Almighty. I'm ecstatic to love that God, and I know we are all His children.

Chapter 38

FULL CIRCLE

It's Tuesday morning, a beautiful crisp early fall day in 2007. Because my office hours don't start until the afternoon, I'm out for a morning walk.

Morning walks are refreshing, a breath of fresh air. The leaves are changing color yet again. Another season is at hand to witness and enjoy. I come out on the driveway through the side entrance. A few leaves have fallen on the driveway. There is a slight chill in the air, and a light blanket of fog in the distance. The fog is gently being lifted away by the powerful rays of the rising sun, like a curtain slowly pulling away for the next scene of nature's drama to unfold.

A few steps into my walk, I'm reminded of my knee injury exactly two years back. It was exactly to the day, on a Tuesday morning when it had happened. I became so completely submerged in my thoughts of what had happened that my pace picked up. The routine of this walk in my neighborhood has always been the same. Two miles, forty minutes, up the hill, on the curved, flat road, around the next cul-de-sac and then down the hill and back home. Nothing has changed in the landscape. I see the same houses, the same sprinkler systems and the driveways, though the shrubs and the trees have grown. The squirrels are still at play, the family of deer graze nearby and the sun rising in the eastern sky.

What is different today in the walk was the thought of the Dear Lord in my mind, dearer than ever before. I revel in my faith in the Almighty God, and my complete surrender to His countless blessings. Somehow I was paying less attention to the scenery than the discussion with the One inside me. *Thank you* and *thank you* kept on coming one after another. Each heartbeat was His blessing and each breath was His Grace.

The walk continued and as I moved forward, I peeped backward into the beginning of my life. Each step forward reminded me of complete and total surrender. The way I was forced to a standstill by my knee injury was fresh in my mind.

Getting closer to home today was painless and easy, physically of course, but my mind was also at ease because today the walk was an acknowledgement of how I have healed physically and spiritually.

After I came home, I relaxed and read the newspaper headlines for a few minutes, showered and got ready to go to work.

At the office, my first patient Mrs. Downey came in for a Physical exam. A fifty-eight year old pleasant Caucasian lady, Mrs. Downey is always smiling, and she takes excellent care of herself.

"Hi, Mrs. Downey, how are you?"

"I'm fine, Dr. B. How are you?"

"I'm fine. Thanks for asking. What brings you here today?"

"I came for a checkup. I had knee surgery three weeks ago on my right knee. It's still swollen and painful."

I thought to myself, *what a coincidence. I have been thinking about my knee surgery all morning.*

"What happened to your knee?" I asked.

"I had a torn medial meniscus, Dr. B. Dr. Kaplan did arthroscopy repair. I was on crutches for two days and I'm still taking the painkillers. Those strong painkillers make me sick."

I paused for moment. *Oh! My God, I had the same surgery two years ago. She is still in pain after three weeks.*

"Let me examine your knee." Her right knee was swollen. There were three rounded swollen tender areas about an inch in size over each wound. The range of motion of the knee was reasonable but restricted.

"When will the pain and swelling get better?"

"Mrs. Downey, it seems you're healing, albeit slowly. It may take a couple more weeks."

"Yes, Dr. B., I'm going through physical therapy. My appointment with the orthopedic surgeon is next week."

I finished examining her, and she got off the exam table and sat on the chair. "Mrs. Downey, we'll take blood for all the necessary tests for your physical exam and my nurse will call you back in one week."

"Thanks, Dr. B."

I saw her come out of the exam room with a limp. She walked the hallway in my office slowly, favoring her leg in pain. I stayed quiet, standing still, watching her limp in pain from the surgery. I had an identical surgery two years ago and was blessed with a painless recovery. I prayed for her healing.

Why was I given a preferential treatment? Mrs. Downey is a nice lady. I'm just like anybody else. Thousands of patients get this procedure done on a daily basis. To this day, it has been an unbelievable, incomprehensible experience for me.

Chapter 39

HOW IT CHANGED ME

Two years have elapsed since the surgery on my knee. My practice of medicine has shifted its gears from pure medical care to faith-oriented medicine, and I have a much better rapport with life, God, and my relationships with everyone.

I had an interesting experience with another patient in the office. Mr. Tabb, a sixty-eight year old Caucasian came to see me for a pre-operative consultation for knee replacement surgery. Mr. Tabb is a high school principal, a bespectacled jolly man, with a mustache and a long white beard that hangs almost to his chest, a red face and white teeth stacked close to each other, making him a perfect Santa Claus.

He underwent the knee joint replacement for osteoarthritis and came back to see me on the fourth post-op day.

"Dr. B, I don't feel good." He paused and started again, "My chest feels heavy. It feels tight, as if I'm not getting enough air." Sitting on the chair in the exam room across from me, I saw the ashen gray color of his face, a deadly pallor that loomed over his usual beefy red face. He looked anxious.

"Mr. Tabb, let me examine you and get an electrocardiogram first, and then I want you to get a lung scan right away."

"What's going on, Dr. B? Do I detect a sense of urgency?"

"I'm concerned; you may have a blood clot in your lung. It's a serious matter. If left untreated, it could be fatal." I could see the look of concern on his wife's face as she sat next to him. Her lips quivered and her face lost its color.

His electrocardiogram revealed sinus Tachycardia—a fast heart rate of one hundred and eighteen beats per minute, much faster than the normal seventy-two to eighty beats per minute. He went to the radiology department for a chest CAT scan and pulmonary angiogram. In less than an hour, a call from the Chief of radiology confirmed my suspicion of multiple blood clots in Mr. Tabb's lungs. He was sent directly to the emergency room for IV blood thinners and admission to the hospital.

Mr. Tabb stayed in the hospital for three days and was subsequently discharged on blood thinner injections and tablets. The following day, he came to the office for a follow-up. "You saved my life, Dr. B"

"God saved your life, Mr. Tabb—I didn't."

He smiled and shook his head, not happy at my answer and asked, "How long will I have to take these injections in my stomach?"

"It takes three to five days to transition from injections to pills. How are you feeling?"

"I feel much better. The tightness in my chest is almost gone. I'm not short of breath, but I still feel tired."

"That's normal. You had a serious condition, Mr. Tabb. It could have been fatal."

"You saved my life, Dr. B. I mean it."

"God saved your life. I didn't."

He laughed and said, "Don't give me that bullshit about God. You saved me. I know He is out there somewhere, but you were here. You diagnosed the problem promptly. Thank you."

He would not let me credit God, so I continued, "Next week we need to repeat the PT/INR tests to check your blood for the blood thinner level." The PT—Pro Thrombin Time test measures the time the blood takes to clot. It should be two to two and a half times the normal because the blood is thinner, so it should take longer to clot. The INR or International Normalized Ratio test has become a standard of care in the last decade.

He walked out of the exam room, looked back, smiled and said, "See you next week."

Mr. Tabb came to see me in the ensuing few weeks for his blood tests and continued to progress well.

Six weeks into his recovery, he asked me, "Could I take a vacation? I'd like to visit my family in North Carolina, and the drive is about seven hours."

"You can go as long as you keep your legs elevated and take frequent breaks and drink lots of water. Don't forget to take your blood thinner medication."

"Dr. B, you think now that I'm fully healed from my surgery, the blood clots in the lungs are gone? You know, you saved my life."

I looked at him and opened my mouth to speak, but before I could say any thing he interrupted me, as if reading my mind.

He raised his hand and shook his head. "Don't you start that God shit with me again. I know who saved me. You were there."

"Mr. Tabb, I know where the credit is due. My belief tells me that God saved your life. I can't help it. That is how I feel. I just did my job."

"Well, maybe, but it happened through you. Anyway, Dr. B, have a Merry Christmas."

We smiled, looked at each other and understood where we stood on God and Life.

Chapter 40

DOOR WIDE OPEN

Throughout this book I wanted to share a true-life experience of what happened to me with my surgery and how it changed my life. It was like a dream, a commingling of emotions that led to faith. The book will not be complete without this last chapter, which is the essence of this whole experience.

Morning walks have become my favorite time to converse with the Dear Lord. I'm alone with nature and these are very special moments. Today is another beautiful fall day and I'm out in the neighborhood on my usual routine. I look at my knee and the way it has healed. The thought of the whole experience fills my heart with gratitude. My eyes fill up at the thought of how I have been blessed.

But I'm sad for not being Lord's best student. Today, I'm an emotional wreck and I don't know why. I slowed down and don't feel like going back home. I want to have some more conversations with God today. I want to thank Him for all what has happened from the deepest part of me, with all the love I have in me. It seems selfish to me how I have been touched by the Lord and I have done nothing for Him. I want to pray for His forgiveness. I want to tell Him again how I feel about all this.

Deeply submerged in my thoughts, I stood on the winding road leading to our house. I gaze across the landscape at the changing colors of the leaves as the beautiful colors of nature's tapestry suddenly come into view against the deep blue sky, the magic kingdom of my Lord in full glory.

At that point I froze, mentally and physically, and lost awareness of my surroundings. Standing still, I whispered *I'm sorry, Dear Lord, I am really sorry. Please forgive me.* I sobbed. My legs became wobbly and my body lacked energy. I slumped onto the asphalt road. My head between my knees, I sat and cried, asking for the Lord's forgiveness again and again.

"Come on in, my son. Why are you sitting over there?"

I thought I heard someone calling me.

Not seeing anyone, it felt as if I were daydreaming. I looked around again, and there was no one around. *What is going on?* I paused for a moment and heard the same voice again.

"Come on in, my son. Are you afraid? I am right here."

This voice was soft yet authoritative, loving yet firm, dreadful yet consoling. Either I was going crazy or my faith was calling me. I felt scared, shaky and tremulous.

My heartbeat raced until I heard the thumping in my chest. My breathing was rapid and shallow, and I felt dizzy and lightheaded. I panicked. *I am going to faint. What is going on? Where am I? Oh, my God, I need help.*

Gathering some courage, I said, "Oh dear Lord is that you I hear?" Nervously I waited for a reply, while anxiety and fear enveloped me.

"Please help me," I said.

"My son, the door is wide open. You want to come in?"

"Come in there with you? How is that possible? Dear Lord, I am not worthy of this."

"Come on in, and I'll take you with me on this journey of faith."

"Dear Lord, what will I have to do?"

"My dear son, have no fear. Surrender to My will and have faith in Me. Don't be afraid. I am here with you."

"Dear Lord, I'm not worthy of this. I have sinned all my life. I have been abusive; I have walked away from the meek and the sick. I have not been charitable enough. I have done all wrong things." I started sobbing uncontrollably.

The Lord said, "I know everything about you. I know all the good and all the bad you have done, and I know what you have been through. You have endured so much, but your faith in Me has never faltered. I'm proud of you, my son, and I have come here to take you and show you a new direction."

I got up and started walking slowly in the direction where the voice had come from. The path was deserted; leading nowhere, yet my mind was at peace with the unknown destination.

"My son, you always believed in Me and kept your faith strong as a rock. I saw your devotion and love for Me ever on the rise. Despite all the troubles, trials and tribulations, you kept Me in your heart. You surrendered to My will. When no one was there to hold your hand, you asked for shelter under My wings. You trusted in Me, my son, I have been watching you since you came to be you.

"I forgive you, My son."

As I listened to all this, I fell on my knees crying, sobbing with both hands covering my face.

After a few moments I pulled myself to my feet in a lighter state of mind, feeling deep inner peace, but I was extremely fatigued. I broke down again and again. Looking up, I said, "Lord, Thank You! Thank You.

"Please keep the door open. I am in."

Thank You! Lord.